Set Free

Harlan D. White &

Dr. L.D. Holmes

Copyright © 2023 JARRETTS Publishing House

All rights reserved.

No part of this book may be reproduced, or stored in a retrieval system, or transmitted in any form or by any means, electronic, mechanical, photocopying, recording, or otherwise, without express written permission of the publisher.

ISBN: 979-8-9881137-0-6

Printed in the United States of America

DEDICATION

To those who know the tyranny of addictions and their destructive power. May the words of one who has walked your walk, speak to your future.

ACKNOWLEDGMENTS

Thank You Avery Atnip for a wonderful cover design.

Special Thanks to Ryan Martin and Esther Luttrell for technical assistance and encouragement.

A heartfelt thank you to Gemma White. Without her permission this work would never have moved forward.

" Let your hopes, not your hurts, shape your future."

Robert Schuller

Introduction

A good friend and a good cup of coffee always makes for a good day.

It was one of those good days that my friend Harlan and I decided we would write a book. He was a fledgling poet, and I, a fledgling writer. Neither of us knew much about writing, but just felt we had a story we wanted to share.

Harlan was a Vietnam vet, with numerous scars from the war, both physical and emotional. He was also a recovering alcoholic who had managed to win his personal war over addiction.

I had the privilege of knowing both sides of his journey. The addiction side was one with its own set of rules. Those rules kept him in a state of abuse, upon both mind and body that few outside the recovering alcoholic can imagine. He tried many programs to defeat the addiction, only to fail time after time.

I will wait for you to hear Harlan's story of recovery, as only he can tell it. Maybe you will find a part of your story in his.

The words of this introduction are in a very real sense a confession. You see, Harlan finished his part of the book, but it seemed like I could never find the time to give attention to my part.

There came a day in our relationship, which changed everything. My friend called and asked if we could meet for a brief time. It was during this meeting he revealed the disease of cancer had come for a permanent visit. I remember when he made the decision to forgo any treatment, and trust God and His ultimate plan. He never flinched or backed away from his absolute confidence in The God who had delivered him from the addiction to drugs and alcohol. He credited much of his positive outlook to a wife who never left his side. She had endured the alcohol and drug days. She had also celebrated the days of recovery. In all ways, she was his greatest cheerleader, nurse, and confidant.

It was an early morning phone call that told of his passing peacefully into the hands of Jesus. The funeral followed. The book was forgotten, fallen by the wayside of procrastination and busyness.

It was not too long ago, as I sat reading Harlan's part of the book, that I felt it just had to be completed. So, here it is. I hope you will enjoy getting acquainted with my friend and personal hero, Harlan White.

Remembering. (Harlan's Story)

"The year was 1965. We met for the first time in a dark wooden garage on South 10th street in Saint Joseph, Mo.

It was sometime before I was with her again, but I found myself thinking about her more and more each day. Entering the military, I worried about living without her. To my great relief, she was waiting for me in Southeast Asia when I arrived.

We experienced the war together, and I found myself including her in all my plans as I returned to civilian life. As the years with her went quickly by, it became painfully apparent, I was far more faithful to her than she was to me. But my love for her knew no boundaries.

In desperation, I sought professional help time and time again for an escape from her evil grasp.

It was now the year 2007, a broken and destitute man, having exhausted all available forms of therapy and treatment, and no hope for the future; I went to The Woods on Wanamaker. It was at this Church on a Sunday morning I listened to Pastor Holmes declare a message of hope and restoration for a world of lost and hurting people, through the blood of Jesus. I had avoided this moment all my adult life, but with nothing to lose, I responded to the invitation to the altar. With a cloudy and a crackling voice, I half whispered these words; God, if you are really up there and can hear me, I'm dying from this addiction. It has a grasp on me that permeates my body and soul. You are my last recourse. If You are really up there, and you really do care, please help me! He was, He does, and He did!

He really was listening to my anguishing cry for help. Furthermore, He did actually care, and as Pastor Holmes and Dan Donaldson knelt beside me at that altar, God in His love freed me from those chains of alcoholism. It's been eight years now I've been free. Not a slip or a sip! To God, be the glory."

Harlan White, 2015

(Harlan White passed away three years later. For eleven years he celebrated his freedom and shared with hundreds, God's power to transform).

CONTENTS

	Dedication	iii
	Acknowledgement	iv
	Introduction	v
	Remembering (Harlan's Story)	vii
1	If Not Now, When?	Pg#1
2	Fear Demands Control	Pg #8
3	In Pursuit of Control	Pg#13
4	Search For What You Have Lost	Pg #19
5	Moving Through Barriers	Pg #25
6	"Easy" Is A Trap	Pg #30
7	Choices	Pg #40
8	Scars Of Hope	Pg #51
9	Cracking Eggs	Pg #58
10	Don't Forget to Remember	Pg #66
11	Passing The Test	Pg #76
12	The Crossroads of Faith and Healing	Pg #81
13	Words Unspoken	Pg #89
14	Introduction To Harlan's Poem's and Thoughts	Pg #93

1 IF NOT NOW, WHEN?

"Doing what we intuitively don't want to do, is the only way we will ever get what we really want."

L.D.H.

It's always a good idea to know where you're going. In fact, your destination becomes secondary to any journey in which you lack good directions.

Most of us can remember the days before the wonderful GPS. (Global Positioning System) For thousands of years, travelers journeyed by looking to the sky. The sun, moon, and stars were their navigators. But today we have the magnificent GPS. It has proven indispensable for anyone traveling to an unfamiliar destination.

Many years ago, while living in Texas, our family planned a vacation to Oregon, the State where I was raised and still had friends and relatives. The first day on the road I made numerous wrong turns. (I have to confess I am geographically challenged) Seeking an answer, we stopped at a hardware store where I purchased a compass. Not just any compass, mind you, but a super compass that touted its ability to get you to wherever you could possibly ever want to go. Let me also add, it was far more expensive than what I thought a good compass should be.

But I needed help, and this looked like a viable solution. In my anxious attempt at finding the answer to my navigation problems, I rapidly tore into it, ripping the package in my haste. Noticing all the small writing on the back of the package, I thought it might be well to read what it had to say. As I slowly pieced it back together, these words appeared." To adjust your compass for optional use, begin traveling due North. Your compass will automatically adjust." That compass never did work properly, mainly because I could never find "due North."

It was from this experience that I have since promoted a more sensible solution for the geographically challenged. Instead of being limited to four directions, (North, South, East, and West) try six directional methods. Straight ahead, Straight back, Up, Down, Left, Right!

On a more serious note, there is a life lesson to be learned. "To get to any desired location, you must have good directions." This is true if you are traveling by plane, train, car or ship. It is also true if you are trying to navigate through all the obstacles' life is going to throw your way.

Knowing where you are going, how you will get there, and what you need for the journey is called preparation. Preparation gives you self-confidence as well as that sense of direction you want and need. In addition, we all require a morality guide.

A good moral compass will do two things for you. First, it will help you to stay on a positive spiritual and moral course. In addition, it will give you a unique ability to handle life's situations. This is individual empowerment.

With that in mind, let's look at this idea of power. Not the kind of power which money buys, or position or authority often demands, but rather a power which supersedes all of these.

This power will help you when you experience the road blocks, dead ends and detours of life. Indeed, you will encounter many situations which attempt to dissuade and discourage you as you navigate your personal life's journey. How you handle these obstacles, or allow them to handle you, will determine to a large extent your joy, sense of peace and ability to adapt to changing situations.

Our direction, not our intention, will determine our destiny. Which brings us to the question we should always be asking ourselves; Is my direction in sync with my intention? A well-worn phrase which still holds true today is "The road to destruction is paved with good intentions."

You will recall in my friend Harlan's story; his direction seldom matched his intention... Thus, he failed time after time in attempting to defeat his addictions.

It was only after he totally surrendered his difficulties, shortcomings, and addictions to God, that he became a candidate to receive a power that would eventually change his life. With that in mind, let's take a moment and look at what "total surrender" looks like from a spiritual perspective.

Using a military illustration, picture two armies in battle. The moment comes when the commander of one army knows the battle is lost. The white flag is raised and the battle pauses. I use the word "pause" because the surrender of one army to another is incomplete until an agreement is reached, and all weapons are surrendered. So, it is, when you realize you cannot win a personal battle. It might be a habit that debilitates, an attitude which precludes a closeness you desire, or, like in the instance of Harlan White, an addiction that's controlling you.

Only after you "totally surrender" your situation, let go of the battle, stop relying on your strength and begin to trust God will the victory come. This point should not be lost; the one you surrender to must have access to power which you do not have, nor can you find or claim for yourself.

Only God's Son, Jesus Christ, has that kind of power and ability.

Many of you can identify with my friend Harlan. He had tried everything within his power. Program after program, after program, only to meet with dismal failure. Will power and self-determination are wonderful attributes, yet they cannot defeat all the enemies which come your way.

Please understand, I am not saying when you totally surrender something to Christ, that the problem/situation is instantly taken care of. After total surrender, things will be different, though. The battle is no longer yours to engage or win. The word total includes "without reservation." Surrender cannot be conditional because that would mean you still exercise some control.

Hear the words of Jesus; "But seek first His kingdom and His righteousness; and all these things will be added to you. Therefore, do not be anxious for tomorrow; for tomorrow will take care of itself. Each day has enough trouble of its own." (Matthew 6: 33-34) "Come to Me, all who are weary and heavy laden, and I will give you rest. Take My yoke upon you, and learn from Me, for I am gentle and humble in heart; and you shall find rest for your souls. For My yoke is easy, and My load is light" (Matthew 11: 28-30).

Edward Deeming, an American engineer, professor, and management consultant said, "Don't inspect the product, inspect the process." You can never "inspect" change into your life, you must build and live the change you want. Indeed, there is a process, that you must embrace and give yourself to.

Let me assure you, there is a road map to spiritual power that initiates change and empowers positive forward momentum.

To validate this point, let's look at a few chapter verses from The Book Of Acts. "And gathering them together, He commanded them not to leave Jerusalem, but to wait for what The Father had promised, which, He said, you heard of from me; for John baptized with water, but you shall be baptized with the Holy Spirit not many days from now" (Acts 1:4-5). "And when the day of Pentecost had come they were all together in one place." (Acts 2:1)

Note if you would, the first step towards success in any endeavor is to follow the instructions. This is true whether you are putting together a cake or a life. In the afore-mentioned verses, they were in the right place, with the right people, at the right time.

I think we can even go so far as to say, it would be nothing less than foolish thinking, to believe that God is going to bless any of our endeavors when we are in the wrong place with the wrong people at the wrong time. God will not bless dysfunction.

Next notice in Acts 2:2 "and suddenly, there came from heaven a noise like a violent rushing wind."

Whenever noise becomes all consuming, it tends to drown everything else out, and we find ourselves focusing only on the noise. In the case noted in Acts 2:2 it was a way to not only get the attention of those waiting to hear from God, but to compel them to listen to nothing else.

On the opposing scale, noise can drown out God's voice. The noise of things, busyness, and self-centeredness can become so loud that you find yourself absorbed in the very thing which keeps you from hearing God when He speaks. Yes, that God can speak above this self-imposed noise is unquestionable; the point is, if you indeed want to hear God's voice, you must take charge of the things which are drowning His voice out.

Have you ever heard someone say, "God is just not hearing or answering my prayers." Maybe we are focusing too much on "things" than we are on God. It could even be we are too busy to take the time to be silent, and give God an opportunity to speak in such a way as for us to hear.

The apostle Paul speaks to this very issue of self-absorption. "It is obvious what kind of life develops out of trying to get your own way all the time: repetitive, loveless, cheap sex; a stinking accumulation of mental, and emotional garbage; frenzied and joyless grabs for happiness; trinket gods; magic show religion; paranoid loneliness; cutthroat competition; all-consuming-yet-never-satisfied wants. A brutal temper: an impotence to love or be loved; divided homes and divided lives; small-minded and lopsided pursuits; the vicious habit of depersonalizing everyone into a rival; uncontrolled and uncontrollable addictions; ugly parodies of community, I could go on" (Galations5:19-21 The Message).

Perhaps it would be wise to stop here for a moment and ask ourselves, "Is what I am filling my life with working out to my satisfaction? Do my actions and life direction bring me joy or useless disfunction?"

We started by asking what does total surrender look like? I think we could agree that it looks like we are not in charge. We are not living an "If it's to be, it's up to me mindset." Without equivocation, personal responsibility and self-discipline are a necessary component leading to positive change.

If our life is in chaos and without joy or purpose, maybe a good question to ask is; "Whose fault is this? Who created the chaos and less than fulfilling lifestyle I find myself in? Why do I find myself always on the outside of happiness? Why is there so much tension, envy, and anger in my life?"

A wise person once said, "When a parent's heart is changed, a child's destiny is altered. When a politician's heart is changed, a nation's destiny can be altered. When a hardened heart is changed, their destiny will be altered."

As we come to the conclusion of this chapter, I want you to again hear from my friend Harlan with a poem he wrote titled "**Can't Get It Right**."

Set Free

Can't write tonight

Can't say what is there

For every step

There appears to be a snare

I chose a path

All my doing

Still searching

Still pursuing

Learning much

With little gain

Great or small

Mistakes cause pain

Footsteps in the drums of time

Equal bondage freedom chimes

Desolate is the mind which seeks

Escape from its destiny

Marching, longing to be free.

H.D.W.

2 FEAR DEMANDS CONTROL

Where lies the value in a man's life?

How is greatness achieved?

Does killing six million Jews make a mad German

Greater than any one of his victims?

Will the annihilation of an entire Indian

Nation bestow greatness on the one who leads the attack?

Can accumulating millions by the sweat of others

Give a man more value than what little his mother

might have seen in him?

Does the lust for power that supersedes human compassion

Raise a man's true worth even one notch?

The measure of man's worth, his success in life,

his value as a human being is always calculated in what good he

has done, who he has helped, what he has built.

Man is not measured by what he destroys, but by what he constructs!

What he puts back together, what he mends, what he heals, and what he touches with love.

H.D.W.

He was a professional thief. Just the mention of his name stirred fear and anxiety. He terrorized the Wells Fargo Stage Line for thirteen years. (1875-1888) From California to New York, his name was synonymous with the dangers of the frontier. He robbed 29 different stagecoach crews without firing a single shot; his reputation was enough. A black hood hid his face; fear was his name; Intimidation was his game. Black Bart, The terror of the Sierra Nevadas.

Fear builds invisible prison bars around hopes and dreams. It communicates the possibility of failure, and all too often keeps us from taking the necessary steps to positive change and success. In fact, I think it would be fair to say, fear kills more dreams than failure ever could. Notice the following analogy about fear;

F alse

E vidence

A ppearing

R eal

Henry Ford said, "One of the greatest discoveries a man makes, one of his greatest surprises, is to find he can do what he was afraid he couldn't do."

Many can remember when the world literally shut down. Children did not go to school, parents stayed home, churches closed their doors and fear ruled the day. Economies crashed, lifestyles changed, freedoms taken for granted revoked and relationships in every sphere strained. It has been called the great pandemic of 2020.

It was during this time of fear and anxiety that many learned a hard truth; adversity never bends to our demands or desires, but actually charts its desired course!

One of the great lessons' history recorded during those days was; How you handle adversity and unprecedented challenge says much about what happens after the adversity wanes.

When things eventually returned to a semblance of normality, many found themselves captive to the demon of fear. Even though by most standards, the world was deemed safe once again, some did not feel personally secure. In many instances, they refused to believe reality. For this group, things would never be the same. Fear had captured and changed them.

Today, if you find yourself in a state of fear or anxiety of which you have no real control, consider this: Adversity can make you stronger if you accept it and begin adapting. Accepting and adapting to any out-of-control situation gives you the ability to move forward. You are no longer captured by fear, but liberated by your choice to not allow whatever you are going through to define you. It allows you to accept your difficulty and move forward. It is in moving beyond your limitation invoked by fear that you begin to discover things hidden from you because your fear was obscuring them.

Remember this; Adversity and fear can only exist in an environment in which you choose to be a victim. When you select the avenue of accepting and adapting, you are in a very real sense saying, "I refuse to allow this difficulty to make me less than the person God has created me to be." No one has been created to be a prisoner of fear. The key, I believe, is to not allow fear and anxiety to get into your spirit, the place where moral and spiritual decisions are made. It has been said, "ships don't sink because of the surrounding water, but because of the water that gets into them."

Harlan White captures the essence of this in his poem:

CHOICES

There is, in every thought, a decision to be made.

There is, in every hand, two ways it can be played.

There is, in every lie, a reason to be sad.

There is, in every question, an answer to be had.

There is, in every story, two ways it can be told.

There is, in every journey, a fork in the road.

H.D.W.

Whatever you do, don't allow the presence of fear and doubt to dictate your life. As Harlan stated, you have the power to choose.

You may be at one of those "forks in the road" today. Determine to lean on God and seek His direction as you move forward. He has the power to help you walk past your obstacles, as you begin to find you can indeed do what you thought you could not! Fear is an addiction which seeks to control not only your choices, but your life in its entirety. When you allow fear to rule the day, you have already surrendered the battle. You have already learned you cannot lose if you have already lost!

Notice how Harlan describes this debilitating syndrome in his well-written expose':

Compulsive Reality

When an addiction is young, its owner is strong!

As the addiction grows, its owner weakens!

As the owner weakens, and the addiction grows, a transfer of power occurs.

It's owner's loss of power will be commensurate with

The addictions increase in strength.

Never, will there be a balance of power, for the two cannot coexist!

One or the other by their very nature must and will always,

Without fail, conquer the other!

H.D.W.

Remember Black Bart, the masked terror of the frontier? His name was Charles E. Boles. A mild-mannered druggist from Decatur, Illinois. He was so afraid of horses he rode a buckboard to every stagecoach heist.

As a wise Statesman once said, "all we have to fear is fear itself."

3 IN PURSUIT OF CONTROL

"Of all men's miseries the bitterest is this: to know so much and have control over nothing."

Herodotus

A MONSTER was created! In my mind, he was conceived.

From hell, he got permission to grow and to deceive!

And though I knew much better

to this, I did agree

Feed me, said the monster! To this, you must agree,

For are you not obligated to feed that which you've conceived?

And though I knew much better

to this, I did agree

The MONSTER grew much faster than you would believe

By now, to me, he could lie, and he could deceive.

And though I knew much better

to this, I did agree

Leave! I told the MONSTER, for you are not a part of me.

No! Roared the MONSTER, my home is where I was conceived.

And though I knew much better

To this, I did agree.

The MONSTER grew so large inside of me, as did his hellish greed

That I spent wasted years trying to meet my MONSTER'S need.

And though I knew much better

to this, I did agree

I have nothing left to give you, all my thoughts you now control

The MONSTER said there still is something that has always been my goal

NOW I WILL REQUIRE YOUR SOUL.

And though I knew much better......

H.D.W.

We live in an anxious world, and it all too quickly becomes a monster we try to control. School shootings, road rage incidents, drug culture demanding control, and even terrorism on our front porch. And we could add to the list, political and moral polarization, tangled race relations, Christianity, under attack, endeavoring to understand woke culture, family struggles, financial insecurity, health concerns, coming to terms with new terms. Well, there just seems to be no end to the list!

Could it be the core of our problem is the "list?" It affects and integrates itself into every sphere of our life, without permission or focused thought. It lives with us and touches everything, from our outward look on life, to how we treat others. Furthermore, it worms its way into our thought process and invariably begins to dictate what we think about, talk about, and act upon.

This Monster list has a well-known cousin by the name of worry. When worry comes to visit, it unpacks its bags of stress, uncertainty and doubt. I believe it was Corrie Ten Boom who said, "Worry does not empty tomorrow of its sorrow, it empties today of our strength." Jesus reminds us, "Give your entire attention to what God is doing right now, don't get worked up about what may or may not happen tomorrow. God will help you deal with whatever hard things come up when the time comes." (Matthew 6:34 The Message)

I think it would be fair to say, if you let any list or unnatural emotions control your thoughts and actions, you will miss out on many of the good thing's life has for you. Trying to control the unknown is nothing short of attempting to control something in which you actually have no real control.

The description for the word worry from the Greek New Testament is "To divide." It divides you from reality and often creates a personality you do not recognize or even like.

To worry about something you cannot change can push you in the direction of irrationally. Of course, to do the same with something you can change can also push you into the sphere of the irrational. If you can change something, just do it and stop worrying. For most of us, worry Is the attempt to control the unknown!

Worry, in and of itself, is, on average, non-productive. It is non-productive because it has no destination. That is why it tends to be a constant companion. Worry is a lie which says it has the answers. It whispers, "just spend enough time commiserating with me, and you will discover a path towards relief and insight."

Because worry has no real destination, it can easily become a "stewing without doing" companion. Solomon, speaking from a position of insight, says," Anxiety in the heart of a man weighs it down, but a good word makes it glad." (Proverbs 12:25 NASB)

Speaking on the perception of life's difficulties, my friend Harlan has this to say; In his work titled:

The Sword and The Cross

The sword was worn from battle, that was plain to see. It lay upon a table marked.....immortality.

With curious hands, I touched the edge...it opened up to me.

There, upon that table, I witnessed all eternity.

All the battles ever fought and all those yet to be

Pointed back to just one day...the day of Calvary

A form I saw upon a cross. The cross became a sword.

The blood that dripped from that sword became a living word

The word became a fountain and offered me to drink

I touched the blood to my lips. It said to me,

All life and all death depend on Calvary.

H.D.W.

Maybe that is part of our problem regarding worry, we tend to wear down from the battle we cannot win and forget the battle that has already been won! As Harlan so righty said in the poem we just read, "all the battles ever fought and all those yet to be, pointed back to just one day, the day at Calvary."

For the Christ follower, Calvary is the key which unlocks our eventual victory over self-defeating worry. Calvary reminds us how unnatural worry is. Animals and plants don't worry. In fact, we could say, mankind is the only part of God's creation that does not trust Him naturally!

Looking at worry as unnatural reminds us it is nothing more than a developed habit. The good news is, bad habits can be broken!

With little effort, we can make the worn-out truism "Worried Sick" a reality. As someone wisely said, "It's not what you eat, but what eats you that debilitates."

Once again, the writer of Proverbs provides some helpful insight. "Trust in the Lord with all your heart, and do not lean on your own understanding. In all your ways acknowledge Him, and He will make your path straight.... It will be healing to your body and refreshment to your bones" (Proverbs 3:5-8 NASB).

I close this chapter with the testimony of a once prominent member of a church I pastored many years ago.

"It all started with nothing much more than the proverbial "wing and a prayer." We structured our start-up business like Matthew 6:33 ("But seek first His kingdom and His righteousness: and all these things shall be added to you"). We decided early on to not allow the pressures of the business to interfere with our church life and responsibilities. God blessed our business. After just three years, we found lack of money was no longer one of our constant companions. It was not that we were getting rich, but we were doing quite well financially. Our problems started when I bought our family a boat. We thought It would be a great way to relax and enjoy family time together. It was not long before we found ourselves spending weekends on the water and at the marina. The weekends were perfect for boating, yet at the same time slowly squeezed out our church attendance, and the fellowship with other believers. Like the frog in the kettle, our spiritual life and the economy both started slowly changing. I sought answers from my friends at the marina, who in turn introduced me to "mister alcohol." He closes his testimony with these true but difficult words," we need to get back...we really need to get back."

Eventually, he did "get back", at the cost of the sale of a boat and the complete restructuring of his life and heart priorities.

Remember, God is in the "get back business." He can take our dysfunctional, worry obsessed and even bad decisions and help us start anew. All we have to do to start the process is to...ask!

4 SEARCH FOR WHAT YOU HAVE LOST

"Losing Teaches you something."

Travis Smiley

Have you ever lost your zip and zest for spiritual things? I'm not talking about backsliding, or turning your back on God or the Church, but rather about "cooling off" in the spiritual arena of life.

When you begin to cool spiritually, spending time in God's Word loses its appeal. Church attendance and worship becomes a mere habit to be observed rather than a spiritual adventure to be enjoyed. Prayer becomes a 911 default, and the things of Christ no longer inspires the way they once did. Spiritual dryness becomes a spiritual desert, where your thirst for other things becomes more compelling than your thirst for God. Oh, you still walk, talk and live as a Christian, you're just not as involved or excited about spiritual things to the same degree as you once were.

Somewhere something happened. Maybe it was something at the time which seemed insignificant and did not immediately register on your spiritual radar. It could have been a painful situation in which you asked God for clarification and help, only to feel bereft of His interest. Pain has that ability. It can push us away, or it can push us closer.

Possibly, in the midst of your pain, you looked for a response rather than an answer.

The biggest problem a Christ Follower can be faced with now is becoming comfortable with their new complacency! You feel a bit empty, kind of like you have lost something, and not quite sure if you want to pay the price of finding it again.

If indeed you are there, or you know of someone who is there in their spiritual journey, know God has a path back to spiritual health.

A good starting place is to pray a prayer King David prayed when he realized he had moved away from God.

"Lord do not rebuke me in Thine anger, nor chasten me in Thy wrath. Be gracious to me, O Lord, for I am pining away. Heal me, O Lord, for my bones are dismayed; And my soul is greatly dismayed; But Thou, O Lord, how long? Return, O Lord, rescue my soul; save me because of Thy loving kindness. For there is no mention of Thee in death; In Sheol, who will give Thee thanks? I am weary with my sighing; Every night I make my bed swim, I dissolve my couch with my tears. My eyes have wasted away with grief;"

If David's prayer resounds in your heart, know three things about you and God. First, God is not mad at you for moving away from Him. Know His grace is sufficient for you in your time of spiritual dryness. And remember, God loves you as much today as He did at your greatest spiritual plateau!

The story is told of a young man who wanted to be hired by a lumber company, so he went to the foreman and asked for a job. The foreman asked the young man if he had his axe? Yes, the young man replied. He told the young man to follow him to where many trees were being harvested. The foreman introduced him to Bill, with this admonition; if you can keep up with Bill doing a day's work, you can have the job. The young man viewed Bill with a bit of distain, noting he was an old man. The boy agreed, thinking to himself, "I know I can cut down twice as many trees as this old geezer." So, the two men started cutting down trees. The old man would cut a tree and then the young man would cut a tree. About every few trees, the young man would notice that Bill would stop cutting. At those times, the young man would swing even harder, thinking this was his chance to get ahead. Hour after hour went by, and at the end of the day, the foreman came and counted all the trees. Bill had twice as many trees as the young man. What, how? Said the young man. "I worked twice as hard, I never rested, I just kept cutting and kept cutting." At this point, Bill asked, "can I see your axe," and he held it next to his? "Son," the old man said, "you never did stop to sharpen your axe. You can swing away, but it will take you forever to cut down a tree with this dull old thing."

I fear the reason some of us find ourselves in a high and dry spiritual desert is because we do not slow up long enough to sharpen our spiritual axe. We all need a "Bill" in our lives to remind us, it is not how hard we work, but how sharp we keep our axe!

My friend Harlan captures the essence of what it means to keep one's axe sharp.

Pressing On

My vulnerably made me fearful.

My fear turned to anger.

My anger, turned to rage.

My rage forced me to find help.

In help, I found God.

In God, I found hope.

In hope, I found life.

In life, I found love.

In love, I found the part of me that, I thought, was missing.

H.D.W.

Harlan says it well! Our vulnerably always takes advantage of our weaknesses. Often, instead of looking for an answer, we look (or opt) for a response. Anger, rage, and disappointment in self and God, throws cold water on our spirit. We "cool off", not out of desire, but rather out of a seemingly necessary defensive response.

In the book of Second Kings, chapter six, we find a similar problem with some of God's chosen. The story revolves around an axe that was lost. Listen to the story and see if maybe you find yourself identifying with some key areas.

"Now the sons of the prophets said to Elisha, 'behold now, the place before you where we are living is too limited for us. Please let us go to the Jordan, and each of us take from there a beam, and let us make a place there for ourselves where we may live.' So, he said, 'Go." Then one said, 'please be willing to go with your servants.' And he answered, 'I shall go.' So, he went with them; and when they came to the Jordan, they cut down trees. But as one was felling a beam, the axe head fell into the water, and he cried out and said, 'Alas, my master! For it was borrowed.' Then the man of God said, 'where did it fall?' And when he showed him the place, he cut off a stick, and threw it in there, and made the iron float. And he said, 'Take up for yourself.' So, he put out his hand and took it."

Now, let's travel back to Harlan's poem "Pressing On." Remember, he states, "My vulnerability made me fearful, my fear turned to anger, my anger turned to rage."

Could it be that a spiritual cooling off happens when we are doing all the right things, yet not giving proper attention to the surrounding things? We focus on "cutting down the tree" and forget why we are cutting down the tree. We make some choices about the immediate, paying little heed to the long-term ramifications. Likewise, we become vulnerable to fear and self-doubt. Our fear morphs into anger and rage at self, and perhaps even God.

Cutting trees for a Godly purpose is a righteous thing, but never at the expense of losing the very thing you will need to accomplish your original goal.

Think with me for a moment about the axe head story. First, why was the workman so close to the water? Second, why did he not take better care of the very tool he had to accomplish his task? Maybe he discounted the danger of working too close to the water. Perhaps he was trying to cut more trees than "Bill" and his fellow prophets. Imagine with me; If he had stopped at some juncture of tree cutting and given attention to his axe, perhaps the head would not have ended up in the water!

Today, it could be that your spiritual axe head is in the water. It is gone, and you have no resource to reclaim it. Tree cutting is no longer an option. You are fearful of the future, angry at yourself for being careless with things entrusted to you which you took for granted; you see no way back.

Our young prophet helps us at this point. Note, the first thing he did when he realized he was in trouble was to call out for help. Not just help from anyone, but one who had the power and ability to actually help him. Allow me to add, many times when we find ourselves in trouble, we often seek help in the wrong places. We try self-medication, or choose denial, and maybe even attempt to blame someone apart from ourselves for our failure.

Accepting personal responsibility for where you find yourself, especially if it is indeed a negative place, is the first step toward reclaiming what you have lost.

Few opt on purpose self-destruction. As with the prophet, who lost the borrowed axe head, difficulties usually begin with our not giving proper attention to the necessary. Taking that first step of asking for help is key to restoration. God cannot bless a step that is not taken!

Another lesson our axe head losing prophet teaches, is to be careful about using what you cannot afford to lose. Maybe we could even double down and say, be careful about where you use what does not belong to you. Things like, for example, influence, second chances and positions of power. We could also add to the list, when someone gives you their trust, or places confidence in you. Be careful, for these things do not belong to you, they are only borrowed for a time.

Well, the good news is our tree chopping prophet did call out to one who could help. And help he did. The story tells us he cut a stick (I have never quite figured out why) threw the stick into the water where the axe head disappeared, and it floated.

This is the place where I think we find one of the real lessons of our story. When the axe head floated, note what happened next. Elisha says to the young man," take it up for yourself!" What was lost is now found.

Could it be, we never actually appreciate some things until they are lost? Especially when we know there is nothing we can do to get them back because It is out of our power and control. Then, answering our plaintive cry, we discover God Intervening. He does the very thing we are incapable of and restores what was lost.

We started this chapter talking about spiritual deserts. Three things we know in conclusion; God does not want us to stay in the desert. He knows we cannot survive, let alone thrive there. In fact, He knows there is a good chance we could die in our spiritual desert.

Our challenge becomes one of decision. Are we willing to take that first step out of the desert? If so, you are probably already aware of the step(s) you need to take. What will you do about it?

5 MOVING THROUGH BARRIERS

"Your Destiny Is Determined By Your Choices"

Unknown

Highway to Hell

I thumbed a ride after walking the road,

Should I have walked? Should I have rode?

The destination is the same on the highway to hell.

It twists and turns, and goes mostly down.

There are no steps, there are no towns.

The only signal on the road is a clock.

Tick tock, ticktock.

Should I ride or should I walk?

Tick tock, ticktock.

Your destination is your kind of fun?

When you arrive, they'll say Welcome, son.

When the rest are sitting at the great supper table,

Don't whine and say you were unable

Now is your chance, make your move.

You have the option to win or to lose!

Tick tock, ticktock

H.D.W.

It takes courage to push yourself into places you have never been. To test your limits and to break through barriers. Could it be a willingness to take risks is indeed a grasp on faith?

How you handle your doubt about the unknown and not allow it to intimidate you towards inaction is indeed faith walking in motion! The way you choose to live your life has real life consequences.

We would all like to have the proverbial crystal ball and see into the future. To realize that the decisions we make daily influence and even directs our future, can be demoralizing. We desperately need a guide, a standard which will help to map out that which we cannot see.

The good news is a whole book has been written for just that purpose. Listen as this Book gives the very guidance many are longing for;

"My son, do not forget my teaching, but let your hearts keep my commandments;

For length of days and years of life and peace they will add to you;

Bind them around your neck, write them on the tablet of your heart.

So, you will find favor and good repute, in the sight of God and man.

Trust in the Lord with all your heart, and do not lean on your own understanding.

In all your ways, acknowledge Him, and He will make your paths straight.

Do not be wise in your own eyes; Fear the Lord and turn away from evil" (The Holy Bible, Proverbs 3:1-7 NASB).

The enemy of doing the right thing, like honoring commitments, and giving of oneself without need of return, is called doubt! It is at this point we encounter the great "What If." What if I choose wrong? What if I make a mistake? What if I try and fail?

Perhaps this would be a good place to be reminded that self-confidence is the result of a successfully survived risk.

To illustrate this, let's review what it means to honor commitments. First, to make a commitment is a risk in itself. What if the person or institution you have given yourself to violates your trust? Do you keep your commitment, or does their infidelity give you license to revoke that which you have committed?

I would suggest being a person of your word is where trust and self-worth are born. It is also the birth of character.

I have a friend of many years who has lived this very experience of keeping commitments in the face of misguided trust. Both he and his wife were and continue to be faith walking people.

The problem began when his wife became involved with a group of well-meaning individuals, whose leader was less than trustworthy. Over a period of twelve months, the wife invested over One hundred thousand dollars in the organization, without her husbands' knowledge.

This was accomplished through amassing credit card debt and personal loans. When the organization eventually blew up and was exposed as a scam, my friend's wife was devastated.

She confessed her transgression to her husband and proposed a divorce as a penalty for her lack of sound judgement. My friend, though terribly hurt and disappointed, refused to follow through on her suggestion. His response was, "when I married you, I made a promise to you, my family, my church and myself, that for better or worse, through sickness and health, till death I will keep my commitment to you."

They eventually were able to work out the massive debt, and today are a faith walking couple. In a very real way, this was because of a Godly man choosing to honor a commitment in the midst of despair and disappointment. Did he have good reasons for walking away, absolutely. Just because a reaction to any situation is a possibility, does not mean it is necessarily the right thing to do.

As Harlan noted in his poem Highway To Hell, "The only signal on the road is a clock, ticktock, ticktock. Now is your chance, now make your move. You have the option to win or lose."

Indeed, eternity's clock is ticking for each of us. How we capitalize on our choices speaks to our eternal destiny.

When the late Nadine Stair was 85 years old, she was asked what she would do if she had her life to live over again? "I'd make more mistakes the next time," she said. "I'd relax. I would take fewer things seriously. Likewise, I'd take more chances. I would climb more mountains and swim more rivers. I would eat more ice cream and fewer beans. I would perhaps have more actual troubles, but I'd have fewer imaginary ones. You see, I'm one of those people who live sensibly and sanely hour after hour, day after day. Oh, I've had my moments, and if I had it to do over again, I'd have more of them. In fact, I'd try to have nothing else. Just moments. One after another, instead of living so many years ahead of each day. I've been one of those persons who never goes anywhere without a thermometer, a hot water bottle, and a raincoat. If I had it to do over again, I would travel lighter than I have. If I had my life to live over, I would start out barefoot earlier in the spring and stay that way later in the fall. I would go to more dances. I would ride more merry-go-rounds. Not only that, but I would pick more daises" (Bits and Pieces, January 5, 1995, pp. 13-14).

To do less is to play the devil's game. One of the greatest mistakes in life is to play it safe; to never risk seizing the opportunity to reach beyond your grasp.

There comes a time in our journey of faith when we must make the commitment to trust God, more than our intuitive reasoning. In its simplest form, faith is relying on God. Faith is not about being an optimist or a pessimist. It is not debating about the glass being half full or half empty, but rather that the glass is held firmly in God's hand.

So today, refuse to believe in a risk-free journey, where the thrill of living is traded for the safety of existence. Being defeated is a temporary condition, giving up is what makes it permanent.

6 "EASY" IS A TRAP

"The greatest danger occurs at the moment of victory."

Napoleon Bonaparte

Genesis: 3

Would we be in this mess, if Adam had confessed and just said,

"'Oh Lord, I've sinned. You made me master of all life upon the earth and in the skies and in the seas. Like Yourself, did you make me?

From dust, I was made, and from a rib was my wife made. You did all this successfully. But, what I don't understand is how after we've been so close, You can hold one mistake against me?

You made the garden and put me in charge and said, "don't eat of that tree," but you also made the snake who set me up for what was soon to be. I didn't know death or sin or shame. I didn't know right from wrong, and with one mistake, You cast me out. That seems a little too strong.

I've done well with all You've given and all my responsibilities. I don't think it's right for you to condemn me, my wife and every one of my seed. I made a mistake. I made a bad choice. A bad moral choice, indeed. But You are Divine, and I am not. That's a lot of difference to me.

Now You blame my wife, You blame the snake and put the rest on me. I admit my part. I now know wrong, and it all seems wrong to me. To blame all three of us and all people ever to be! You put that tree in front of us when all things You could see.

You knew what would happen and how it would go. How it would affect history. Isn't knowing good from evil punishment enough for eating from one bad tree? Remember in the mornings in the garden we'd walk, when it was only You and me? You loved me so much, we shared so much.... now death is what it must be?

If You were a man and I were God, I'd create some mercy for me. I would say that I forgive, and that forgiveness would replace that old tree. Then I'd write Genesis 3."

God answered Adam quietly. "Adam, I agree. I cannot undo what has been done, but My Son will write Genesis 3. He'll fill the void and bridge the gap that now exists between you and Me. And like you, Adam, He'll face a test from a different kind of tree.

A price must be paid for what has been done. That's the way I caused things to be. I did it that way because as each price is paid, another step is made toward perfect eternity. You're the beginning of something much greater than yourself. Much greater than you can conceive.

When you tasted the fruit of knowledge, you opened a door for Me. This battle between good and evil has raged through eternity. In you, I created a battlefield where I can conquer evil completely. When I created "choice" I created something that was new to even Me!

We'll be together forever, Adam, you just wait and see. We've been temporarily separated by death because of that 'ole tree. One day, we'll be united again on a hill.... Calvary....your seed My Son and Me."

H.D.W.

National elections are always a time of political intrigue and stress. There are those who believe beyond any doubt their candidate(s) are much better suited for the cause than the oppositions.

Unfortunately, many times after the political race for positions of power and influence, there are those who feel discouraged and maybe even deceived by the one in whom they had placed their trust. They were so sure in their judgement, only to find they may have been badly mistaken.

What should we do when those in whom we have placed trust and confidence fails us? Perhaps Bruce and Bubba can help us untangle our feelings of neglect and marginalization a bit.

Bruce and Bubba went deer hunting on a cool fall day. Bubba shot a trophy buck. They started to drag it back to their truck. As they were pulling it by its hind feet, they found it's fur and antlers kept catching on the briars and brambles, making it difficult to pull. Another hunter seeing their dilemma suggested it would be easier to pull the deer by its rack of antlers. After some moments of discussion, they decided that their hunting friend was onto something. As they were dragging the deer by its rack, Bubba said,"Ya know, this is a lot easier to drag now." "Yeah, but we sure are getting a long way from the truck," replied Bruce.

The moral of Bruce and Bubba's story is, don't forget where your truck is located!

A thought to consider, when it comes to those in whom we place trust and confidence, maybe we have been placing our hope for better days and easier ways in the wrong place. I think we can all agree that self-deception is the greatest deception.

The apostle Paul addresses this issue of looking for someone else to make our way easier in Ephesians Chapter Six. Beginning in verse ten, he states:

"Finally, be strong in the Lord, and in the strength of His might. Put on the full armor of God, that you may be able to stand firm against the schemes of the devil. For our struggle is not against flesh and blood, but against the rulers, against the powers, against the world forces of this darkness, against the spiritual forces of wickedness in the heavenly places."

Note, if you will, the battle, though engaged here, is actually a battle being waged in places we have never trod. Paul describes the battle as against "spiritual forces of wickedness in the heavenly places." Looking at our difficulties from that perspective seems to beg the question, what is a Christ follower to do when the battle is raging on our doorstep?

Going back to the start of this discussion, we made mention that "easy" is a trap. With that as a focus, allow me to suggest a few things we can do in the midst of the battle.

First, be strong in your stand for moral righteousness.

I have a person quite close to me who is in her last days of undergraduate college work. She intends to continue her education in the medical field. She also has a young man who she thinks the world of, to the point of discussing a possible marriage. The situation they are facing is four years of grueling medical school, followed by another number of years of internship before she can begin her practice.

In the culture we live in today, many young people will opt for the easy way of just moving in together and putting any prospective marriage on hold until a more opportune time. Instead, they have mutually agreed there would be no communal living, and no marriage relationship until marriage was a reality.

Will it be easy for them, no! But, they both understand that easy is a trap, which has hidden consequences beyond the immediate. The problem with moral shortcuts is they often cheapen that which was intended for beauty, while at the same time contributing to a lack of trust and self-esteem.

Being resolute and not wavering during times of stress and difficult decision-making situations are, in a very real sense, of paying it forward. We could also say it is a good way to keep your spiritual eye on your ultimate destination.

Going against the grain of "easy" will never be easy! There is a cost involved with every decision we make, especially when it includes our spiritual rhythms and moral values.

For years, I have struggled with balancing my schedule with a planned exercise program. I know what I should do, and even what I want to do, but it is frequently easier to let the hours slide by, until there is just no time to incorporate that workout regimen. I also know I will never have the physical and emotional stamina I desire by simply working out one hour a week!

The same holds true for the one who wishes to feel good about themselves in the spiritual arena. Going to church once a week for an hour is never going to get you to where you really want to be spiritually.

Remember, we are in a "cosmic" battle, and no part of our lives will ever be free from that arena of conflict. The good news is, we are not in the battle without resources. Listen to the words of the psalmist in the 46th division of the book of Psalms.

"God is our refuge and strength, a very present help in time of trouble. Therefore, we will not fear, though the earth should change, and, though the mountains slip into the heart of the sea; Though its waters roar and foam, though the mountains quake at its swelling tide.

There is a river whose streams make glad the city of God, The holy dwelling place of the Most High. God is in the midst of her, she will not be moved; God will help her when morning dawns. The nations made an uproar, the kingdoms tottered; He raised His voice, the earth melted. The Lord of hosts is with us; The God of Jacob is our stronghold."

In our moral quest, there will always seem to be an easier way. This is where we again realize self-deception is so dangerous. It paints a picture we want to see, not what the landscape actually is. Because we have a moral tug to the "easy" we can easily skew the outcome to favor our desired destination.

When God created mankind and imputed the ability to choose, we entered into a journey of choices. Harlan so vividly captures the essence of this in his poem;

Forever and Ever

The scene was solemn and the light just a glow.

I wasn't noticed, no one seemed to know

That I was disoriented and didn't have a clue where to go.

So, faking a smile, I stopped one sad old fellow.

What am I doing, and why am I here?

When he looked up to respond, the hot wind dried his tears.

This is forever

Forever what I asked?

Forever and ever, now tend to your task.

I'm new here, I said, pardon me if I ask

But what is my purpose, and what is my task?

Your purpose is on purpose, you chose to be here,

And as far as a pardon, there's no such thing I fear.

Set Free

Your task is to make ready for the wedding that will be.

You will set placed throughout eternity.

You'll shine each golden plate and polish each cup.

But sir, may I interrupt?

What's all this for?

Forever and ever, don't ask anymore.

What you're doing is your own undoing.

You're here, is that clear?

You were invited to be part of the feast,

But you chose not to hear, they received no R.S.V.P.

You did nothing when you had the chance.

Nothing has produced nothing, so nothing you are.

You're nothing to anyone here.

We're nothing to each other.

Wait a darn minute, you can't do this to me!

You did it to yourself, do you like what you see?

Polish your plates till they shine in your face,

Then look as you set the table and remember

Your choice you made in life

H.D.W.

The easy way is not always wrong, and the hard way is not always right. The question we should ponder is not if something is easy or hard, but is it wise?

"The greatest joys come in the greatest victories, and the greatest victories come from the greatest battles when they are fought in the power and with the power of the Lord." (John McArthur)

Once again, the cosmic battle Paul is alluding to is all encompassing. It engages in battle with the mind, the body and yes, even the spirit which resides within you. Its purpose is to sow doubt, confusion, and despair.

So, that being the place where we sometimes find ourselves, what is the wisest course to follow? The apostle Paul addresses this when he says, "No prolonged infancies among us, please. We will not tolerate babes in the woods, small children who are an easy mark for imposters. God wants us to grow up, to know the whole truth and tell it in love— like Christ in everything. We take our lead from Christ, who is the source of everything we do. He keeps us in step with each other. His very breath and blood flow through us, nourishing us so that we will grow up healthy in God, robust in love." (Ephesians 4: 14-17, The Message)

For a major victory, there must be a solid battle plan. We are instructed to "put on the full armor of God, that you may be able to resist in the evil day, and having done everything, to stand firm. Stand firm therefore, having girded your loins with truth, and having put on the breastplate of righteousness."

In an earlier chapter, we spoke about this thing called truth. When you have questions where there appears to be no valid answers, stand firm in the truth that you do have. For instance, you know that Jesus is the Son of God. You know He lives and reigns in your life today. You know He forgives, heals, and has defeated death. Likewise, you know He is King of Kings and Lord of Lords. You know you are loved by Him, and He longs to have a personal relationship with you.

The things you do know will often be the catalyst which creates new pathways of knowledge and understanding. God never wants to hide truth from you, He just wants you to be mature enough to handle the truth He reveals.

The idea of a "breastplate of righteousness" reminds us that it protects our heart. When your heart desires purity of purpose, it gives you a boldness to attempt things you have never contemplated before. A by-product of the "breastplate" is that it also protects you from unwanted and unnecessary criticism. It was Theodore Roosevelt who said, "it is not the critic who counts, nor the man who points out how the strong man stumbles, or where the doer of deeds could have done better. The credit belongs to the man who is actually in the arena, whose face is marred by dust and sweat and blood; who strives valiantly; who errs and comes up short again and again; because there is no effort without error, and shortcomings; but who actually strive to do the deed; who knows the great enthusiasms, the great devotion, who spends himself in a worthy cause, who at the best knows in the end the triumph of high achievement and who at the worst, if he fails, at least he fails while daring greatly! So that his place shall never be with those cold and timid souls who have never tasted victory or defeat."

Next, Paul speaks about our footwear. "And having shod your feet with the preparation of the gospel of peace."

Good footwear is necessary for any successful endeavor. Having the right shoes brings a sense of stability as well as peace of mind for what lies ahead. Knowing you can walk into any situation, well balanced and prepared is often a big part of many battles.

We are further instructed to not forget our shield. Paul uses the wording "in addition to." It is this shield (faith) which will help you to thwart the schemes of those who want you to fail. You need to become your greatest cheerleader! I speak not about narcissism, but rather about cultivating a healthy self-image. "Flaming darts" are central weapons in satan's armory. Darts of gossip, fake news, betrayal of friends and the exploitation of weaknesses, find their demise when they encounter the "shield." Never go into battle without it!

Finally, Paul speaks about the "helmet of salvation" and the "sword of the Spirit," which is the Word of God.

The helmet protects the eyes (the things you should not look upon) the ears, (the things you should not listen to) and the mouth, (the things you should not speak of) These can pretty well be wrapped up in what we call our mind. It is the mind which is the gatekeeper of the choices we make. The mind feeds our spirit, and our spirit negotiates our moral aptitude.

The sword is the only offensive weapon we have at our disposal. In fact, it is the only offensive weapon Paul speaks of. Because we have the offensive weapon of the sword, we are not to sit by passively in the moral realm of life, but to go on the attack!

The Hebrew Writer describes the sword in this manner.

"For the Word of God is living and active and sharper than any two-edged sword, and piercing as far as the division of soul and spirit, of both the joints and marrow, and able to judge the thoughts and intentions of the heart."

Paul closes out this part of his instructions to us by reminding us to not forget the importance of prayer. Prayer levels the playing field of life and allows us to compete on any level, for moral righteousness.

Remember the words of our good poet Harlan, "you were invited to the feast, but you chose not to hear, they received no R.S.V.P."

7 CHOICES

"Attitude is a choice. Happiness is a choice. Optimism is a choice. Kindness is a choice. Giving grace is a choice. Respecting is a choice. Whatever choice you make, makes you. Choose wisely."

Unknown

We are the sum product of our choices. Although this is one of those truths difficult to escape, we many times wish we could. All, at times, would like that twenty, twenty hindsight that is never offered.

Looking back on history, we can find several people, who, if given the chance, would make some different choices.

In 1936 Joe Schuester and Jerry Segal sold the rights to Superman for $65.

Sam Phillips sold a small recording company to RCA records in 1955 for $35,000. It included an exclusive contract with a young man named Elvis Presley, unknowingly forfeiting royalties on more than a billion records.

There was the high school girl who said to Bill Gates, "It's either me or the computer."

Then there was the economist who suggested selling Wal-Mart

stock in exchange for K Mart stock.

In Germany, a bank robber pulls out a gun and demands money. The teller says she needs to see his ID. So, he pulls it out, takes the cash, leaving his ID behind.

There was a farmer having difficulty with skunks. He designed and made a live trap.

And, who is not aware of the hapless husband who paused to long before answering when his wife inquires, "Do I look too fat in this?"

Our good poet Harlan checks in with this poem about:

Choices

"There is in every thought, a decision to be made.

There is, in every hand, two ways it can be played.

There is in every lie, a reason to be sad.

There is in every question, an answer to be had.

There is in every story, two ways it can be told.

There is in every journey, a fork in the road."

In every situation, there is a right way. Knowing the right way and going the right way are two different quadrants in life.

At one time, wristbands were popular with the inscription "What would Jesus do?" The question was fair, but they quickly became too uncomfortable to wear. Maybe we just need to be reminded, it is not always easy or popular to do the right thing.

To illustrate this point, let's look at a few scenarios. You go to the mall with shopping on your mind. When parking your car, you accidentally hit another parked vehicle, doing some minor damage. No one sees the incident. Do you leave a note, or just leave?

A cashier gives you back too much change. Do you smile and give it back, or just smile and walk away?

A friend shares a shocking secret. Do you keep quiet about what they have shared, or do you betray a confidence and let others in on the story?

God's Word is faithful to remind us;

"Every man's way is right in his own eyes, but the Lord weighs the hearts. To do righteousness and justice is desired by the Lord rather than sacrifice" (Proverbs 21:2-3 NASB).

Without doing injustice to God's Word, I think we could even say, it is easier at times to sacrifice than to do what is right.

We have all encountered the person who lives for events that produce an emotional high. Their life revolves around waiting and anticipating the next exciting event, which they hope will boost them up for another day. The difficulty with pursuing emotional events, and their ensuing euphoria, is that they tend to feed the baser and more desirable parts of our psyche. They just seldom have staying power.

To adopt a lifestyle of living each day to its fullest brings with it sustainability. You can grow in character and spirit consistently, as you make seemingly small decisions, which leads to personal satisfaction. I think this is what it looks like to have roots.

Take for instance the root system of a tree. The roots not only provide nourishment, but also stability. They hold the tree sturdy in storms and times of drought. Oh, the tree may lose a few leaves and branches to the howling wind, but it remains, stationary, because of its root system.

Humanly speaking, we all have roots. It is from this root system that our personality traits as well as our genetic makeup is formed. It would seem safe to say that the fruit of your life is often determined by the roots of your life.

We should also note, the roots that receive the greatest care and nourishment are the ones which will produce the greatest fruit. It has been well documented; we are what we eat. A junk food diet will never sustain the rigors one encounters in our journey through life, and its unavoidable hazards.

You probably noted, we are using the multiple description of roots rather than the singular. This is because we have a multiplicity of growth areas in our lives.

One of the greatest roots you can and should nourish are your spiritual roots. It is out of this root system that the important things of life are born. Character, integrity, and your future well-being finds its foothold in this arena.

Many moral dilemmas of our life and culture would cease to exist, if we just stopped pursuing "Christlikeness" and spiritual righteousness. There would be no such thing as "temptation" if we extinguished the moral and spiritual values which tends to follow the person with a moral mind set! The quiet truth is you can achieve a certain modicum of peace if you are just willing to surrender the moral attributes which guides spiritual morality.

Some questions to examine might be; What do I want from this life? What am I willing to pay? What do I expect in the next? It is difficult and morally impossible to surrender moral roots and yet embrace a future of eternal bliss! If one pursues a life of "self-rule," where Christian attributes are ignored, nothing you achieve will ever be enough. You will always be pursuing something which you can never obtain. The book of Haggai, in the Old Testament puts it this way;

"Now therefore, thus says the Lord of hosts, consider your ways! You have sown much but harvest little; you eat, but there is not enough to be satisfied; you drink, but there is not enough to become drunk; you put on clothing, but no one is warm enough; and he who earns wages, earns wages to put into a purse with holes" (Haggai 1: 5-6).

A 14-year-old boy by the name of Jason Lehman penned these words;

It was spring

But it was summer that I wanted

The warm days,

And the great outdoors

It was summer,

But it was fall, I wanted

The colorful leaves

And the cool, dry air.

It was fall,

But it was winter I wanted,

The beautiful snow,

And the joy of the holiday season

It was winter

But it was spring I wanted,

The warmth

And the blossoming of nature.

I was a child

But it was adulthood I wanted.

Set Free

The freedom

The respect

I was twenty

But it was thirty, I wanted

To be mature

And sophisticated.

I was middle-aged

But it was twenty, I wanted

The youth,

And the free spirit,

I was retired,

But it was middle age I wanted,

The presence of mind,

Without limitations.

My life was over,

But I never got what I wanted.

For those desiring a life where Christ plays a major role, be careful to not fall into the trap of ignoring inconvenient truth. You can care for someone without agreeing or embracing their particular values, or lack thereof. Yes, there are consequences for ignoring God's moral absolutes, but it does not mean we should demean or dismiss a person caught up in a moral situation, or even an outright sin!

All of us, regardless of our past, can begin growing a new root system. Judging someone who is caught up in unrighteousness will normally only intensify their rebellion. Be assured, their very actions will dispense whatever condemnation is necessary. Ours should never be to take the position of judge, but rather intercessor. The Christ-follower can relax now, for your love and caring of another person will never change God's moral absolutes. At the same time, your love, and caring may just bring them into a place of self-discovery, and eventually salvation.

Remember what roots do! They eventually produce fruit. The kind and type of fruit produced will be determined by which roots have received the greatest nourishment.

Bitterness can be a fruit too often displayed, even in a Christ-follower's life. Bitterness is a deep, spreading anger, typically operating beneath the surface. Unfortunately, it eventually pushes to the surface. Actions, like refusing to forgive, displaying a critical attitude, having a short temper, and always seeing the negative in every situation, are some of the fruits which will eventually manifest themselves.

Bitterness usually begins with a legitimate sense of moral outrage. It is a deep-seated anger that feels morally justified. This is the trap that is so easily sprung!

I was twenty-six years old and serving in my first assignment as Pastor of a local congregation in the State of Texas. I had never met my birth father. My oldest brother knew of him and had given me his name and local Texas town where he lived. After moving in and getting settled, I thought I might explore the possibility of introducing myself to him, if indeed I could locate where he lived.

Looking at a map (Those were days before the introduction of the GPS) I discovered the town where he lived was only 49 miles (ca. 79 km) from where we were now living. I got his address from a regional telephone book (this was before the internet) and proceeded to his home. The address I had obtained was his workshop, located next to his home.

He was busy working on some metal project when I walked in but paused his work when he saw me. I had never thought through what I would say when this moment came. I introduced myself and told him I was a pastor of a local church some forty-nine miles distant. I then plunged into my story of always carrying his name in my wallet, with the intent of one day looking him up, believing he was perhaps my birth father. I shared a brief few bits of historical information, such as my mother's name and address and the date of my birth. I stated that I was aware he had been stationed at a nearby Naval base.

His immediate reaction was one of denial. He went into a long litany about how what I had always believed could never have happened. I assured him that I was not there to cause any trouble or distress, but just wanted the opportunity to lay eyes upon him. I watched as his shoulders slumped, and he uttered these words. "I always knew this day would come. You look exactly like my son, who is two years younger than you. I am going to ask you not to introduce yourself to my family. If you did, my wife would know instantly who you are."

Trying to understand, I assured him I would not bother him again, but if he would like to know more about me and my present family, it would be welcomed. I left him with my business card, in hopes of after the shock had worn off, he might desire to make contact. I followed his life from a distance, keeping my word that I would never cause him or his family any embarrassment or trouble. Forty-eight years later, I read his obituary in the local newspaper. He never attempted to make contact. He lost out on the journey of two daughters who excelled in numerous areas. Today, his "accepted" family would be able to look and see how their children also excelled. In fact, today there are two registered nurses, one teacher, two physicians, one speech pathologist and two yet waiting in the wings to decide.

For the next few years, the fourth commandment and Father's Day were a bit of a struggle. I would generally just push my feelings to the corner of my spirit and attempt to ignore the disappointment.

I share this personal story with you because I want you to know, we do not have to live with disappointment and bitterness. There came a day in my life (I cannot find it on the calendar, but I can in my spirit) when I discovered I could move on, by faith in three things.

First, came the knowledge God was aware and working. As I reflected on the last fifty plus years, I found God had given me an earthly father at each stage of my life development. I know the people who study the mind and actions of people would readily say, I was looking for that father figure. Perhaps they are right. If so, it certainly was a sub-conscience action on my part. I choose to believe God was fulfilling that empty place in my heart because of His love for me.

Second, I began to grasp the reality that no one has a perfect father. We are all of a fallen nature and must have the redeeming power of God to find abundant life here on earth. God has allowed me to witness the devastating effects of a child whose father was less than stellar. I realized I could have been one of those who were indelibly marked with a different kind of bitterness. A bitterness only the betrayed know.

Third, the reality of my personal forgiveness has worked in such a wonderful and powerful way. God has forgiven so much in my regard, which now allows me to give forgiveness regarding others, even my father!

One last thought about bitterness. We often want someone to be punished for our hurt, humiliation, and disappointment. This is a quagmire for the Christ-Follower. How much punishment is enough? How much revenge can we extract from another before we ourselves are diminished? And the real question; Could they ever "pay" if they wanted to? It is far better to give it up and let it go. Allow God to take care of those things in which you have no power or influence. The only way you will ever successfully deal with your bitterness is to grow some new roots of compassion and forgiveness. Remember, it is your root system, your tree, and your fruit!

I close this chapter with the affirming words of my friend Harlan:

Eternal Father

No darkness can hide me from you.

If I took up the wings of an eagle,

You would already know my course.

Even in my doings

My soul reports back to you.

Your greatness is unfathomable

All my life, you have shown me a straight path.

You have led me to a road upward

That I avoid the shoals underneath.

Who am I that you who made the cedars of Lebanon

Should call me to mind?

Your greatness is beyond the understanding of one lifetime

You have been gracious to me.

Tho the thistle has been in the drunkards hand

And the proverb in the fool's mouth,

Yet, You have shown me mercy.

Never have I suffered from need or begged for bread.

I cannot see Your face, but I can feel your hand upon me.

Set Free

In times of trouble, You are always there.

In times of danger, Your footsteps precede mine.

Your protection is with me day and night,

Always you are by my side.

You govern the universe by Your will,

While the heavens display your handiwork.

In the sanctuary of your glorious night,

The planets and stars maintain their paths.

The seasons of earth rotate in order,

As do the seasons of man.

Until the silver cord has snapped.

And I have traveled to my eternal home

Until the dust returns to earth and my spirit returns to You,

I will praise you for my redemption

And trust in your steadfast love

HDW

8 SCARS OF HOPE

"Ask God what lesson on healing He would prescribe for you."

Unknown

Most have at least one on their body! And most have at least one on their heart. They are usually produced by events we would rather forget.

We are told "scars" are evidence of healing, and in a very real sense they are. Every scar has a story! Reality pulls us to the story when we see the scars. Many would say they are a mark on our memory, and all too often on our very spirit.

Remembering some things can be paramount in their importance. Holidays, anniversaries, birthdays, and special occasions which we want to celebrate are intricately woven into our very lives. (Just forget a birthday or anniversary of a special person in your life) Life teaches us, the things we do not celebrate we tend to forget. Most have found a good calendar to be a valued companion. We go so far as to take pictures, record videos and even scrawl notes to help us remember. I think we do this because, like scars, every memory has a story.

My co-writer Harlan was an avid fisherman. One night, after a great day of fishing, he had a dream. It was one of those dreams he did not want to ever forget, so, being a writer, he wrote about his dream.

PARADISE LAKE

In my dream I stood at the edge of an unearthly magnificent lake. The water so clear it reflected the sun.

Sparkling crystals of aqua blue water took my breath away.

In the distance, I saw a dock and marina filled with brand-new fishing boats. I reached the dock after a lovely walk and met one white-haired gentleman.

He smiled, and I caught a twinkle in his eye as he greeted me.

Good morning my fellow fishing friend, calling me by name, welcome to Paradise Lake.

Trying to hide my surprise, I returned his smile, and asked him about this heavenly place.

He began a story about the lake that started at the beginning of time. This lake was created for real down to earth fishermen, those like you and me. There's plenty of fish of every kind. The minnows are six inches long.

We have Bass, Largemouth, and Browns, Crappie, Walleye, Cats of all kinds, Bullheads, Channel, Flatheads and Blues, Muskie, Pike and Salmon.

You name it, we have it too.

I asked about the tackle and what a man would use.

He seemed amused by my choice of words, such as what a man would use, but politely continued and reached for a pole lying on the dock.

We use these, he said, presenting a golden rod made of a material totally unfamiliar to me. The length expands and contracts depending upon its use. The line on that reel never breaks, and those hooks have never been known to bend or dull.

When I inquired about such boats, he led me a few slips down the dock. That's not fiberglass son, that's father-of-pearl. It never cracks. A rock struck solid won't even leave a scratch. Seeing no motor, I naively asked, what makes her go? You do, he said. She'll go as fast as you will her to go. I noticed the bow had no numbers, and then to my surprise, my name fully written in silver was scrolled upon her side! Sure is, he said, that one's yours. It's been here since the beginning of time.

Embarrassed by my excitement, I said, can we take it for a spin? His voice softened as he spoke, not today, my friend.

I noticed other boats with other names nearby: - - Simon, James, John- - -

With his hand upon my shoulder, he led me off the dock. You'd better go now; you don't belong here yet.

With great reluctance, I complied and started back down the shore. One last question, sir, how will I find you when I return?

Again, I saw that twinkle in his eye. Ask for Peter, I'm well known around here. Then we said goodbye!

As the alarm clock rang, I sat up with a smile, ready to rise and shine. What is it my woman asked? Oh, nothing honey, I replied. I was just thinking about an old friend of mine.

H.D.W.

(In the year 2018, Harlan claimed his father of pearl boat, picked up his golden fishing rod and set sail on the lake called Eternity)

Scars, yes, we all have them. But as Harlan so aptly reminds us in his poem, scars will all be erased, on God's heavenly shore.

Maybe this would be the place to examine what we are doing with our scars, while still residing this side of heaven. Because we are the sole commonality in their creation, we do have some options.

We can remember, and rehearse their creation, allowing the pain of the past to persuade us that healing has not occurred. Thus, those scars become ugly reminders of battles engaged and lost. They become a focal point in the creation of prolonged low self-esteem and worth. Thus, they will keep us running in the same rut day after day, wondering, is there no justice or relief?

Harlan White could have been that person. He certainly had his scars, some of which he has already shared with you. Addictions, twisted priorities, tarnished relationships, always running, but never having a goal or destination.

Or you can choose the path he chose. Accepting responsibility, asking forgiveness from God, and those closest to him. Experiencing transformation and enjoying the ability to forgive himself, and others. That kind of experience will always provide a whole new perspective about scars.

In its simplest terms, it comes down to moving forward, or continuing a downward spiral. YOU are in control, and it is your option to select. Will either option be easy? Absolutely not. It is your choice, though, and one will prevail and rule over the other.

Allow me to share one of Harlan's "transformation stories."

After being released from prison, the law of the State said he could never again possess a driver's license. His local church was located in the Capital City. By its very nature, several State employees and members of congress were affiliated with the church.

One of those individuals became aware of Harlan's story of spiritual transformation. At the time, Harlan and his wife Gemma were serving as the prayer coordinators of the churches monthly all night of prayer. (He would always place a note on the entry doors of the church for those who had the assignment of the late and early morning prayer slots, which read "Any problems call the White House" with his personal phone number.)

The individual watched and observed Harlan month after month. One day, during a casual conversation, Harlan shared with him his inability to possess a driver's license. One conversation led to another, which eventually led to Harlan presenting his plight and personal spiritual journey to a congressional committee.

At the next session of the State Legislature, a proposal was presented to allow individuals like Harlan to obtain a driver's license, with the caveat that a driver's personal vehicle be equipped with an alcohol monitoring device. That would be the only vehicle that could be used by said driver. The legislation passed and Harlan was the first to receive the new restricted license. The very next day, he drove to his favorite fishing spot!

As stated earlier, scars can be evidence of healing, but not all healing is healthy healing. For the healing to be healthy, positive and spiritual change must occur. As Harlan would testify, without this change, new wounds will occur, only to eventually heal in an unhealthy way.

For those who are struggling with "ugly" scars, allow me to share with you a story of challenge and victory from God's Word.

The setting and background is found in the Old Testament Book of Joshua, Chapter 1.

Before this, the children of Israel had wandered for forty years in the wilderness, never possessing their God given inheritance. Just before the opening of Joshua Chapter 1, Moses, who had wonderfully led the people of God out of Egyptian bondage, has died. The leadership now falls to his successor, Joshua. As their new leader he was to do what Moses, one of the greatest leaders of all time, could not do, and that was to lead the people of Israel into the promised land. As I relate the story, picture yourself in Joshua's shoes. Just as an aside, Joshua was acquainted with some scars, just as we all are!

"Now it came about after the death of Moses the servant of the Lord that the Lord spoke to Joshua the son of Nun, Moses servant, saying, Moses My servant is dead; now therefore arise, cross this Jordan, you and all this people, to the land which I am giving to them, to the sons of Israel. Every place on which the sole of your foot treads, I have given it to you, just as I spoke to Moses. From the wilderness and this Lebanon, even as far as the great river, the river Euphrates, all the land of the Hittites, and as far as the Great Sea toward the setting of the sun, will be your territory. No man will be able to stand before you all the days of your life. Just as I have been with Moses, I will be with you; I will not fail you or forsake you. Be strong and courageous, for you shall give this people possession of the land which I swore to their fathers to give them. Only be strong and very courageous; be careful to do according to all the law which Moses My servant commanded you; do not turn from the right or the left so that you may have success wherever you go. This book of the law shall not depart from your mouth, but you shall meditate on it day and night so that you may be careful to do according to all that is written in it; for then you will make your way prosperous, and then you will have success. Have I not commanded you? Do not tremble or be dismayed, for the Lord your God is with you wherever you go."

Now, place your scars in Joshua's story. Maybe you will hear your story and future.

"Now it came about after the death of my dreams, that the Lord spoke to me. Your past has no hold on your future. Now get up and move on. Not just move on but move according to my plan for you. I have given this plan as your inheritance. Every place your foot treads, I will bless and bring to good. From the crushing defeats of yesterday, to the glorious promises of new and beautiful things, I will be with you. Nothing will stand in your way. Just as I have been with the redeemed in the past, so I will be with you. I will not fail or forsake you. Be strong and courageous, for you will be a testimony to my strength and loving kindness. Many people will follow in your footsteps, and find victory for their life, just as you are now finding. Only be strong and courageous; be careful to allow My Word to be your bulwark. Keep it before you, night and day. Do not look to the left or the right but move forward into the promises I have prepared for you. This is the path in which you will find success and fulfillment for your life. My goal is to make you prosperous and to help you become the person I have created you to be. Do not tremble or be dismayed, for I, the Lord your God, is with you wherever you go."

Scars, yes, we do indeed all have them! The excellent news is scars and their stories are incomplete. They will always be in a state of development, until we meet our Master, face to face. Until then, allow God's Spirit to help turn your scar stories into stories of victory.

9 CRACKING EGGS

"Strength does not come from winning. Your struggles develop your strengths.

When you go through hardships and decide not to surrender, that is strength."

Arnold Schwarzenegger

Humpty Dumpty sat on a wall

Humpty Dumpty had a great fall

All the King's horses and all the King's men

Couldn't put Humpty together again.

I enjoy cooking as a hobby. In my cooking journey, eggs often posed a bit of a challenge. Cracking them without breaking the yolk and keeping small parts of the shell out of the cracked egg was always a pain. I eventually mastered the art, at the expense of numerous eggs and many unwanted servings of scrambled eggs.

Along the way, I learned some things about the humble egg. First, once you crack an egg, you cannot un-crack it! Second, once you scramble an egg, you cannot un-scramble it! And of course, if you never crack the egg, you can never enjoy the myriad of opportunities presented, and even though you cannot un-scramble an egg, you can make a beautiful omelet.

The original Humpty Dumpty nursery rhyme found its way into the family nursery in 1870. It was James William Elliott who included it in a number of other nursery rhymes set to music. There were some people at the time who thought the rhyme might have been alluding to King Richard III of England, who was humpbacked and defeated at the battle of Bosworth Field in 1845.

Regardless of its origin or intent, it does serve to pose a question for the Christ-follower. What happens when we are the egg that gets cracked? This human egg cracking experience is known by numerous descriptors. Loss of innocence, being unwilling or unable to take responsibility, unresolved anger, loss of trust and yes, even, the desire to self-medicate.

Harlan explains it this way in his poem "**Mirage.**"

It rolled, and it rolled till it rolled right by.

When I was high, I laughed. When I wasn't, I cried.

Once it seemed internal infinite in scope

Then it occurred too late, the mirage of the Dope.

What I thought lay ahead was not what was there.

What I once saw as Hope at a closer look was despair

It rolled, and it rolled till it rolled right by.

As age consumed my youth, I continued to fly.

I soared above Life, with no altitude.

Most of the soaring done in a bad mood

It rolled and it rolled till it rolled right by

It rolled right up to the time to die.

It rolled way beyond the time to ask why.

I laughed when I was High, when I wasn't, I cried.

H.D.W.

There are many things that have the ability to break us. Of these, ego stands stark and tall. Yes, when we think we have all the answers, and life would be so much better if more people were like us, breaking is inevitable. Whenever we make everything about us, breaking will occur. When we see ourselves as an island, with no real need of anyone or anything else, breaking is in the offering. When we refuse to forgive and choose to hold on to the hurt, breaking is invited to the party.

I suppose in one respect, breaking is not only inevitable, but necessary. After all, the egg was never intended to be left unbroken. The truth is, only in the breaking is real worth discovered. If the egg is never cracked, the intended meal can never be served.

At the expense of pushing the "Humpty Dumpty" theme too far, could it be in one sense we are all eggs, fragile, and easily cracked? In addition, as much as we abhor the thought, it seems "cracking" is often the necessary process for creating something better.

I cannot imagine anyone saying, "I'm eagerly awaiting to be broken." Yet, as many will testify, brokenness does not ask for permission, space or proper timing, but visits on its timeline.

Brokenness, by its very nature, will change a person. How that change matures is entirely up to the person. Many will see brokenness as an irredeemable loss, while others will see it as a new beginning.

Pride and insecurity are powerful partners. Pride refuses to accept offered change, while insecurity keeps it at bay. Because pride is centered in the deep pleasure of self, it pushes against the possibility of being wrong. Insecurity joins forces and says don't risk the unknown, stay the course of self-promotion.

Humility, or the ability to see oneself as God (and others) see them, is the opposite of arrogance and pride. The strength of a humble person allows them to confront their faults and weaknesses and accept change as an avenue to becoming a more balanced individual. This acceptance of self eventually will produce a sense of true self-worth and positive self-esteem.

Change for the positive good in a person's life is never easy. To say it will be pain free is distorting its direction and value. Most realize without some difficult times; it is nearly impossible to know and appreciate peace and mental well-being. The kind of change necessary for a productive and robust life is where the joy of discovery is found. Without it, there would be no sense of "awe" or the appreciation of something new.

When you refuse to allow humility to become a life partner, you thwart the personal growth potential inherent in all of us. Because you have circumvented God's best, you will never move into His best. The good news is, you do not have to stay where you are. You can at any time turn your heart toward God and allow the change process to begin in the positive realm. After all, it is your life and your road to walk. You even have the opportunity to choose whom you invite to walk with you.

Many see God as an entity who is the arbiter of good and bad. A ruler and scorekeeper, who hands out prizes to those that toe the line and conform to His format of life. Who at the least cares for His creation, but at best does it from a distance.

The following says it so much better than I ever could:

"At first I saw God as my observer, my Judge

keeping track of the things I did wrong, to know whether I merited heaven or hell when I die

He was out there, sort of like a president. I recognized His picture when I saw it, but I didn't really know Him.

But later on, when I met Christ, it seemed as though life we're like a bike ride, and I noticed Christ was in the back, helping me pedal.

I don't know when it was He suggested that we change places, but life has not been the same since.

When I had control, I knew the way. It was rather boring...but predictable. The shortest distance between two points.

He knew delightful long cuts, up mountains and through rocky places at breakneck speed. It was all I could do to hang on!

And even though it sometimes looked like madness, He said "pedal"

I worried and was anxious and asked 'where are you taking me'? He laughed and didn't answer, and then it was when I started to learn to trust.

I forgot my boring life, and entered into an adventure. And when I'd say, 'I'm scared', He'd lean back and touch my hand.

He took me to people with gifts that I needed, gifts of praise acceptance and joy, and they gave me gifts to take on my journey, my Lord's and mine.

And we were off again. But He said, 'give the gifts away; they're extra baggage, too much to weigh.

So, I did…to the people we met. And I found that in giving, I received, and still, our burden was light.

I did not trust Him at first,..in control of my life. I thought He would wreck it: but He knows bike secrets, knows how to make it bend to take sharp corners, knows how to jump to clear high rocks, knows how to fly to shorten scary passages.

And I, I am learning to shut up and…pedal, in the strangest places, and I am beginning to enjoy the view and the cool breezes on my face with my delightful constant companion, Jesus Christ.

And when I'm sure I just can't do anymore, He just smiles and whispers…'pedal'. (Author unknown)

As mentioned earlier, you get to choose who accompanies you on your journey through life. Does your chosen companion add or subtract from your desired goals and destination? Is your companion making life a positive adventure or a thrilling ride into nothingness?

Self-honesty says, I'm the last person I want to try to fool. Every so often, we will have to say no to the good to experience the best. Pride says I can take everyone on my journey. Humility says only those who are a positive influence are welcomed to the journey.

The apostle Paul, of the New Testament, correctly says, "Do not be deceived bad company corrupts good morals" (I Corinthians 15:33 NASB). Indeed, you do become like the people you spend time with. When you look at your closest friends, you look into a mirror.

Harlan captures this thought in his poem "**Melancholy Blues**."

Today is another day. It is raining. The thunder brings back ghosts of another time.

I am strong. But my strength takes me to places I've already conquered. They are few. I will meet life today with expectations. I will do what I must, as honorably as I am able.

I will try, as best I can, to feel. I will try to feel something not associated with anger. I will be the peaceful person I wish to project. However, I will survive. I will overcome all apparent adversities. I will reach inside myself and extract what is required to survive or exist.

I will display love, as I see it, to those closest to me! If I error, I will apologize. I will concur, as closely as possible, to what I interpret as socially correct. I will seek a Higher Power, which I neither know nor understand!

Each year of my life is one trip around the sun. I will make as many trips as are required of me, doing as little harm as I can do to others as they make their journey. If I have the opportunity to help someone along the way, I will do it without reimbursement.

I will experience happiness, joy, peace, and fulfillment. I will be happy, if it kills me! I'm being positive, I'm sure of it! The things I like most are:

BIG FISH

LITTLE KIDS

TALL TRUCKS

SHORT STORIES

LONG NAPS

SKINNY GIRLS

FAT ON PRIME RIB

AND YOU!

H.D.W.

As we close this chapter, I invite you to consider a few thoughts. First, when you are going through "egg breaking" trials, at the point of your deepest suffering and hurt, you are at that point most like Christ! In the midst of your "cracking", you can rejoice because you know Christ also suffered! Rejoicing is not happiness, but rather knowing that you are not, nor will you be defeated.

Learning to rejoice through difficult and trying days soon becomes a spiritual discipline. It reminds you to not quit, give up or back up. In fact, it is at this very place of hardship that growth begins to grow and manifest itself.

Finally, trials, tribulations and, even, temptations have a unique way of drawing you closer to Christ. Never allow personal suffering and difficulties to attack your sense of intrinsic value and worth. You are loved and valued by God as much today as the day you were born. Accept His love and rejoice!

10 DON'T FORGET TO REMEMBER

"Brethren, I do not count myself to have apprehended; but one thing I do, forgetting those things which are behind and reaching forward to those things which are ahead, I press toward the goal for the prize of the upward call of God In Christ Jesus."

Saint Paul (Philippians 3:13-14)

As I mentioned in previous chapters, Harlan White and I decided years ago to co-author a book. If you recall, he finished his portion, while my part went by the wayside of procrastination. After visiting with Harlan's wife Gemma, I received permission to "finish the job."

Harlan has been gone several years now, but his writings serve to keep him alive in so many ways. All of his poems and thoughts, put to words, bear the imprint of a man who was a true cycle breaker in every way!

Following is an "Introduction" to his portion of the book.

(Please note, his complete work will be presented without editorial comment or revision after our shared work is finished)

"Last year I found my way to the Veterans Hospital. What brought me here? The same circumstances that brought you here. Desperation. Frustration. Hopelessness. Oh yes, and one other crucial element, a hero brought me and stayed with me until I had enough information to decide about enrolling in treatment. Someone had been here ahead of me. Do I know his name? I don't think I can remember it. Why did he do that? He understood what you and I understand, but can't find a way to explain or get past.

Let me make this perfectly clear. I hated treatment. I hated every moment. The treatment was more than I believed possible for a human being to endure. In fact, I did not make it completely through my prescribed treatment. Nevertheless, during the months since, I have found something happening inside of me that I can't easily explain away.

Describing that "something" is more than difficult. Maybe I can't accurately define it, but I can say in reflection that it started here, at the Veteran's Hospital. My downward spiral plateaued here. I hit with such force and pain that I could not recover my consciousness for a while. In truth, I didn't know if I ever would.

Since my treatment, I have awakened to my own self-destruction. So, now what? If I do acknowledge that the thoughts I live in; the negative, destructive thoughts that represent my entire thinking process are killing me, I am more horrified than ever because I don't have a clue how or with what to replace them. Where do I begin? Is it too late to change? Is it worth the effort? I suppose my hero thought there was hope.

Today, my self-destructive thoughts do not enjoy as much freedom as they once did. They do come to mind with regularity, but not unquestionably. Where my sure-fire answers to all things resided, I now find the ability to question, to contemplate, to allow myself to take in knowledge. Somehow, I found wonderment and dreams again. Only you can appreciate what a miracle this is.

My bedrock, my innermost foundation, is in the process of rebuilding. Could it be some things are positive? I am not as terrified as I was, day by day. I am escaping my inner world of terror, replacing it with possibilities.

Yes, just like you, I have experienced many tragedies. I mourn the losses of my life. While I am not trying to forget that or diminish those experiences, I am trying to include some other factors. I am practicing another focus. It doesn't seem natural just yet, but there are many things I could appreciate. There are many things in my life that bring a sense of gratitude, when I think to go there. I'm still practicing. I think that I will always be practicing.

Maybe because I am a carpenter, I think of my mind as having a workbench in it. On my mental workbench I have moved some things over that were taking up all the space and I have put some other things on that workbench. Looking here at the other things, I amazingly find some rest and peace. I am learning from the bottom up, that I must find a way to love and heal myself. The principle that I continue to find amazing is this. The only way out of my internal prison is to give-a-little. Give a little each day; don't give away too much, but give away a little every day.

Am I still overwhelmed? Do I still feel too small to deal with life every day? Yes. Yes. Yes. But I am not thinking about that at this moment. I am thinking about giving a little today. That's what this is about. Although I do not fully understand what happened to me at the Veteran's Hospital, I know that something started in me there, and I must acknowledge that process. I have a need to show my gratitude. Maybe it's just plain good manners... I need to say "thank you!" I need to say "thank you" to the hero that brought me here. Thank you for hope, when I couldn't find it for myself.

May you find a stopping place here. May you find a flicker of light in the darkness of your soul. Although you may find this the darkest hour of your life...remember... others have walked before you and we are holding you in our hearts. Holding you in the same hope that someone held us. Holding you through the pain you're feeling right now. Beyond the pain amazing discoveries are awaiting to be made and behind every discovery is a secret! In wonderment and dreams, you will find clues to your secrets."

Harlan reminds us, when we fail to say "thank you" or show gratitude, we become the losers. To bring to mind the things of the past which helped to shape us is to begin to treasurer those life-changing events and memories. Indeed, memories are life's greatest souvenirs. They never rust or tarnish, although they may need to be dusted off occasionally.

History has always held a fascination to me. Because I am an American by birth, American history reads like a novel. Let me say at the onset, I don't necessarily like or approve of all of America's history. At the same time, I am reminded, history does not present itself for my acceptance or approval, it just presents the facts as they were and are.

American history has been lived and thus recorded by individuals who were flawed and at times lacking in integrity and selflessness. Because those who lived and created history were at times flawed, so is American history flawed and far from perfect.

The history of America records some fundamental errors in judgement by both our elected and non-elected leaders. As bad and evil as mankind can become, I believe there is a remnant of Godliness in everyone. I believe the same about our Nation. As bad and perhaps even evil as some in leadership positions have acted, I believe America has some sustaining remnant of Godliness at her core.

When looking back, we all have 20/20 vision. Problems, poor choices, and errors in judgement are clearly seen, in the rearview mirror. Undoubtedly, many of our current and future difficulties could be undone if we could just get a "do over." I am speaking of such things as institutional slavery, wars waged with less than good fore-thought or proper motivation. Electing representatives to places of power without proper vetting, just because they happen to belong to our tribe, and the list goes on.

Add in the mixture fake news, which we have encouraged and allowed to mold our thinking into an image we dislike or approve of, we find ourselves quickly mired in criticism, cynicism, and despair. If we could just go back and get that "do over" things would look so much brighter. But alas because it is history, there are no "do-overs," but that does not mean we cannot do better.

Fortunately, we do have some historical documents which provides for a basis of hope as well as thankfulness. Of these documents, The Declaration of Independence shines bright even in the darkest of times. Note the second paragraph. "We hold these truths to be self-evident, that all men are created equal, that they are endowed by their Creator with certain unalienable rights, that among these are life, liberty, and the pursuit of happiness."

One of the fears I live with regarding America is that it appears we are dividing up into tribes. The Blue tribe, The Red tribe, The White tribe, the Black tribe, the Yellow tribe or the Brown tribe. Somewhere along the way, we have forgotten that none of us had anything to say about the "tribe" we were born into.

The soul and spirit endowed by our Creator reflects no such boundary of tribalism. The problems we face in today's culture are not caused by skin tone or color, but rather by the moral condition of the heart. Real, authentic moral change will occur when the heart condition of humanity is properly addressed.

I suppose it can come down to a question of prejudice. Often, when the word "prejudice" is mentioned, we automatically think of race. It will come as a surprise to some, but there will be no white, black, brown, red, or yellow people in heaven. We will all be the color called "redeemed." Before you fall into the "pre-judging" crowd, think about the following:

Harland Sanders was a 6th grade dropout. Today, there are over 17,000 Kentucky Fried Chicken Franchises. Walt Disney was fired from The Kansas City Star, lacking imagination. Oprah Winfrey was fired from her first television job as anchor. Vincent van Gogh only sold one painting in his lifetime. Jim Carrey dropped out of high school and lived in a van for two years. Stephen King's first novel (Carrie) was rejected by thirty different publishers. He currently has sold over 350 million copies of his books. Bethany Hamilton had her arm bitten off by a shark at the age of 13 while surfing. Instead of succumbing to defeat, she went back to the ocean and her surfboard, and two years later won first place in the "Explorer Women's Division" of the NSSA National championships.

Life contains a myriad of surprises, so be careful who and what you dare judge. In addition, if you are one of those whom some may tend to judge, never allow your personal situation to dictate your future possibilities!

When it comes to Liberty, we all have the right to move up or into whatever dream we decide. But make no mistake, liberty is never easy or cheap. Simply ask a Harlan White, or another recovering alcoholic or past drug abuser.

We say Thank You to our Creator and God when we maximize our potential. When we refuse to say, "It's not worth it", or "I give up." We also say thank you when we remember where we were and where He has brought us from.

In America, we have the privilege of unlimited opportunity to maximize our God given potential. To stretch out our hand beyond our grasp, knowing He will make up the difference, if we are dedicated to His purpose for our lives.

I am proud to be a Christian American. Not because, as I have documented, America is great, but because I am free by national and spiritual design to pursue my destiny in my chosen way. Because America has "solid bones" constitutionally, I need only defeat my own weaknesses to thrive, as I so desire.

Samuel Adams (known as the Father of The American Revolution) said:

"These rights may best be understood by reading carefully and studying the Institutes of The Great Lawgiver and Head of the Christian Church, which are found clearly written and taught in the New Testament."

Patrick Henry (known for his statement to the Second Virginia Convention: "Give me liberty or give me death") said: "It cannot be emphasized too strongly or too often, that this great Nation was founded by Christians, on the Gospel of Christ."

James Madison (Father of the Constitution and author of the Bill of Rights) stated: "We have staked the whole future of American civilization, not upon the power of government, far from it, but upon the capacity of each and all of us... to govern ourselves, to control ourselves, to sustain ourselves, according to the Ten Commandments of God."

Rudyard Kipling made famous the term "lest we forget," in his poem "Recessional." The phrase occurs eight times, and is repeated at the end of the first four stanzas to add particular emphasis regarding the dangers of failing to remember.

God of our fathers, known of old,

Lord of our far-flung battle line,

Beneath whose awful hand we hold

Dominium over palm and pine

Lord God of Hosts, be with us yet,

Lest we forget, Lest we forget.

We find a similar vein in the Old Testament Book of Deuteronomy 4:7-9

"For what nation is there so great, who hath God so nigh unto them, as the Lord our God is in all things that we call upon Him for? And what nation is there so great, that hath statutes and judgements so righteous as all this law, which I set before you this day?

Only take heed to thyself, and keep thy soul diligently, lest thou forget the things which thine eyes have seen, and lest they depart from thy heart all the days of thy life, but teach them to thy sons and thy son's son's...."

Remembering the good things of your journey, and being thankful, often becomes the path to the happiness you so desire.

I fear one of the reasons so many in our culture are perpetually angry is because, no matter how hard they try, they never seem to find a place of contentment and happiness. They perceive and even see it in others, but for whatever reason, it always seems to elude them.

When we can see happiness as a pursuit and not a destination, it can change our personal perspective. When we expect "things" or institutions, or even Jesus to make us happy, we are on a dead-end pursuit.

What is frequently neglected and even railed against is that happiness is an individual pursuit. It is up to the single solitary individual to discover happiness, and once discovered to cherish.

As a pastor, I have had people come to our church looking for spiritual happiness. In short order they become disheartened, and often blame God, the church and yes, even the pastor. The churches' mission is not to make someone happy, but to proclaim the Gospel of Jesus Christ. Jesus did not come to make us happy; He came to provide salvation.

Money, relationships, positions, and possessions will never provide lasting happiness. Happiness is an inside job. Individuals are the only ones with the power to create personal happiness. So, if you are not "happy" look no further than the reflection in the mirror. And maybe, just perhaps, try being thankful for what you do have!

Albert Schweitzer said, "At times, our light goes out and is rekindled by a spark from another person. Each of us has cause to think with deep gratitude of those who have lighted the flame within us."

The following is adapted from a Paul Harvey program called "The Rest Of The Story."

An old man walks down a Florida beach. The sun sets like an orange ball on the horizon. The waves slap the sand. The smell of saltwater stings the air. The beach is vacant. No sun to entice the sunbathers. Not enough light for the fishermen. So, aside from a few joggers and strollers, the gentleman is alone.

He carries a bucket in his bony hand. A bucket of shrimp. It's not for him. It's not for the fish. It's for the seagulls.

He walks to an isolated pier cast in gold by the setting sun, he steps out to the end of the pier. The time has come for the weekly ritual.

He stands and waits.

Soon the sky becomes a mass of dancing dots. The evening silence gives way to the screeching of birds. They fill the sky and then cover the moorings. They are on a pilgrimage to meet the old man.

For a half hour or so, the bushy-browed, shoulder-bent gentleman will stand on the pier, surrounded by the birds of the sea, until his bucket is empty.

But even after the food is gone, his feathered friends linger. They linger as if they are attracted to more than just the food. They perch on his hat. Likewise, they walk on the pier, and they all share a moment together.

The old man on the pier couldn't go a week without saying "thank you."

Set Free

His name was Eddie Rickenbacker. If you were alive in 1942, you probably remember the day that he was reported missing at sea.

He had been sent on a mission to deliver a message to General Douglas McArthur. With a handpicked crew in a B-17 known as the "Flying Fortress," he set off across the South Pacific. Somewhere the crew became lost, the fuel ran out, and the plane went down.

All eight crew members escaped into the life rafts. They battled the weather, the water, the sharks, and the sun. But most of all, they battled the hunger. After eight days, their rations were gone. They ran out of options. It would take a miracle for them to survive.

And a miracle occurred.

After an afternoon devotional service, the men said a prayer and tried to rest. As Rickenbacker was dozing with his hat over his eyes, something landed on his head. He would later say he knew it was a seagull. He didn't know how he knew; he just knew. That gull meant food...if he could catch it. And he did.

The flesh was eaten. The intestines were used as fish bait. And the crew survived.

What was a seagull doing hundreds of miles away from land?

Only God knows.

But whatever the reason, Rickenbacker was thankful.

As a result, every Friday evening this old captain walked to the pier, his bucket full of shrimp and his heart full of thanks."

Don't forget to remember!

11 PASSING THE TEST

"Hardships often prepare ordinary people for an extraordinary destiny."

C.S. Lewis

One of the perils of learning is the inevitable test which accompanies most educational pursuits. We normally like to learn but would rather shun the test which measures what we have retained in our memory banks.

To be clear, we like to "test" we just don't like the idea of being tested. We are, in one sense, a test-oriented people. We test water before we drink it; food before we eat it; air before we breathe it; cars before we buy them; Truth before we accept it, and even relationships before we fully commit ourselves.

Anything worth anything has in some measure been tested. Testing is not a lack of faith or trust, but an exercise of wisdom. It was Ronald Reagan who immortalized the words, "trust but verify."

Testing is normally preceded by a question. To answer any question, one must first take the time and opportunity to prepare. All students realize lack of preparation almost always increases the chance of failure.

Few, if any, would dare trust something (or someone) that has not been tested. When I get on an airplane, I want to know that, not only the airplane has been tested for air worthiness, but the pilot manning the plane has also been tested for his ability to adequately fly the plane safely. When my medical doctor prescribes a medication for me, I would like to know both doctor and medication have been tested in their ability to meet my physical needs.

On a personal level, how we face testing and trials will often make the difference between success and failure. The purpose of any test is to help develop self-confidence and character. We feel good when we successfully pass a test.

Our world and daily commerce tests us regularly. Be it the congestion of traffic on the way to work, or the obnoxious workmate who just will not stop being a thorn in the side. Tests and trials are numerous as well as often necessary. We live in a fallen world and cannot avoid them, nor in some cases, should we.

James, one of the writers in The New Testament says, "Consider it all joy my brethren, when you encounter various trials, knowing that the testing of your faith produces endurance" (James 1:2-3).

I must admit, whenever I have found myself in the midst of a test or trial, I did not envision my goal as obtaining joy. Usually, I was just happy to have survived it. It has been in times like this that I have had to turn to God and say, "I don't understand why this test is upon me, but the one thing I do know is that you have got it!"

When the test lies before us, or we find ourselves in the midst of the flames, it is good to be able to say, this is bad, but it will not crush me. Indeed, when the wind is blowing the hardest, and flames are at their fiery height, it is here that we can remember past trials and tests, which were also bad, but did not destroy us. We survived then and can survive them now!

The apostle Paul writes in The Book of Romans," But in all things we overwhelmingly conquer through Him who loved us. For I am convinced that neither death, nor life, nor angels, nor principalities, nor things present, nor things to come, nor powers, nor height, nor depth, nor any other created thing, shall be able to separate us from the love of God, which is in Christ Jesus our Lord" (Romans 8:37).

In another of Paul's writings he says, "We are afflicted in every way, but not crushed; perplexed, but not despairing, persecuted but not forsaken, struck down but not destroyed" (11 Corinthians 4:8-9).

As I stated previously, I have never gone through a test or trial with the thought that Joy would come to me in any way. Yet, I have discovered there is a simple yet profound way to navigate the tumultuous time of trials. The core of this discovery is found in the New Testament book of James. "But if any of you lack wisdom, let him ask of God, who gives to all men generously and without reproach, and it will be given him" (James 1:5).

The term "lack" means to "not be wanting" in anything. So, in the midst of difficult days, it is our privilege as a Christ Follower to say to God; "show me how to get through this. God, help me find your purpose in this trial." And yes, "God show me how to discover joy". Note, James says God will "give generously." Asking of God for help is not about inadequate faith, but rather one of wisdom!

Our poet and friend Harlan says it this way in his poem, "**Pink Clouds and Purple Skies.**"

Pink clouds and purple skies surround the mountains in her mind.

She closes her eyes.

She is dancing.

The breeze from the top is exhilarating

The wind fills her wings,

She's flying.

Musical currents in time like thermals give lift to her heart.

The sun is shining. Her heart full of joy,

Sings from the highest peak.

She's loving

Without warning, darkness and fear cover her world.

She's falling, twisting and turning. Spiraling out of control.

She looks within herself for an answer. There is none.

Tranquility and peace lay below her in the valley that so quickly welcomes her arrival.

She's lonesome.

Her breath eludes her. Her lungs collapse.

Laying face down, hope trickles from her dreams. She's hurting.

The slightest gust creates a spark.

From a spark, a flame. From a flame, a fire.

She's burning

Feeling again, belonging again. She's living from the mountain, so high to her...

They beckon to climb. She hesitates. She knows...

I'm always on the mountain when I fall

H D W.

Harlan reminds us, it is not on the mountain top that we find a place of residence, but in the valley. The mountain top is beautiful, but it is there where the storms first occur, and the winds blow the hardest. In the valley there is protection from the winds of adversity. It is in the valley where you grow, blossom, create and fully become the person you can love. Enjoy the scenery of the mountain top, but find your dwelling place in the valley of hope and discovery.

12 THE CROSSROADS OF FAITH AND HEALING

"You cannot discover new oceans unless you have the courage to lose sight of the shore" (Unknown).

It has been said, "integrity is one of several paths. It distinguishes itself from the others because it is the right path, and the only one upon which you will never get lost."

This becomes evident when dealing with spiritual things. Irreparable harm has been done by individuals seeking to hijack God's name and reputation for personal advancement, popularity or momentary self-fulfillment. You can see this in the presentation of some of the more outward of the spiritual gifts.

Of these, spiritual healing has played a major role. Televangelists, and popular seeking purveyors of God's Word have often given a less than positive image of the wonderful gift of spiritual based physical healing.

Some mysteries defy explanation. This is no more true than in the realm of Godly things. To even try to understand God is like trying to get all of a room in your hand. You can get some of it, but it is just too big to get it all. So it is with the things of God. We can get some understanding of God in our minds, but He is too big and vast to get all of who He is into our finite thinking process.

For many, Divine Healing has been one of those big things of God which they have never been able to fully comprehend or understand. I do believe some have discovered aspects of the spiritual gift of healing which has helped in their own spiritual journey. Here are a few of those insights.

First, it appears Divine Healing is seldom for a given situation or person alone. There seems to always be a lesson within every lesson on healing, just as there seems to always be an event within an event. We know intuitively when a person is spiritually healed, they will eventually die. After all, dying is simply a portal we walk through to the life called "eternal."

We also know God uses a plethora of ways in which to bring about divine healing. Doctors, technology, medications, prayer, and divine intercession are a few which seem to be mentioned often. Certainly, God has unseen and unheard-of remedies in His arsenal!

It is good to be reminded, God does not restrict Himself to any certain ritual, function, or method. After all, He is God, and all things are at His disposal.

I believe unequivocally, Divine Healing is just as real and possible today, as it was in the days of Christ's time upon earth. Lest we forget, God does not change, nor are his powers diminished by time.

I do know, and have witnessed, that faith often plays a major role in any instance of Divine Healing. At the same time, I must admit, even defining faith itself is difficult to fully comprehend or explain.

The New Testament records 37 different events of Divine Healing. You will find these scattered throughout the Gospels as well as the Epistles of Paul and the Book of Acts.

I want to share one of our friend Harlan's writings, which gives a different slant on understanding the difficult things of God.

Life Is A Poem

Standing in life one day

While looking at the sky

I happened to chance a poem go by.

The poem grew so sad I began to cry

I cried when it was over and as it went by

I cried for the person and their plight

I cried for their situation most of the night

I longed to help and make life better

When they were lonesome I searched for the right letter

What I wanted to say came way to late

For the words of the poem had long since sealed their fate

I'm happy I got this glimpse as it went by,

But to care and not say is to flap and not fly

I cried right up until dawn

Then I cried because it was gone

I cried not for myself but for what

I could not do to make life better for even these few

All of the crying perhaps was in vain....

For why should one cry for another's past pain?

So in the morning my mourning I ceased

I put back the book and erased the crease

I thought of all the poems that would pass me by

I felt for each one, but, this time I didn't cry

Life is a poem as each day goes by

Sometimes we must laugh so we do not cry.

H.D.W.

Many of us have encountered situations like Harlan describes in his poem. We want to help, we feel we need to help, we try to help, yet it seems help is beyond our reach.

Perhaps we are missing the core reason for divine healing. Look with me at the following verses and pick out the one commonality in regard to Jesus'-healing of individuals.

"And it came about that as he was approaching Jericho, a certain blind man was sitting by the road, begging. Now hearing a multitude going by, he began inquiring what this might be. And they told him that Jesus of Nazareth was passing by. And he called out, saying, Jesus, Son of David have mercy on me! And those who led the way were sternly telling him to be quiet; but he kept crying out all the more, 'Son of David, have mercy on me'! And Jesus stopped and commanded that he be brought to Him; and when he had come near, He questioned him, what do you want me to do for you? And he said, 'Lord, I want to regain my sight'! And Jesus said to him, receive your sight, your faith has made you well. And immediately he regained his sight, and began following Him, glorifying God; and when all the people saw it, they gave praise to God" (Luke 18:35-43) NASB.

And then again in Matthew 9:18-22,

"While He was saying these things to them, behold, there came a synagogue official, and bowed down before Him, saying, 'My daughter has just died; but come and lay Your hand on her, and she will live.'

And Jesus rose and began to follow him, and so did His disciples. And behold, a woman who had been suffering from a hemorrhage for twelve years, came up behind Him and touched the hem of His cloak; For she was saying to herself, if I only touch His garment I shall get well. But Jesus turning and seeing her said, Daughter, take courage; your faith has made you well, and at once the woman was made well."

(Matthew 9:18-22) NASB

Note they all exercised faith, but I wonder, could there be another lesson Jesus wants to teach us about divine healing?

If the blind beggar had his sight, would he have reached out to Jesus? Would the woman with the issue of blood exercised faith, and reached out believing Jesus could heal her, if she were healthy?

We can be assured God does not cause disease, sickness, and life's difficulties to bring glory to Himself. We live in a fallen world and disease, sickness, and life altering difficulties will invariably come our way. God can and often does use these very dire circumstances to bring individuals into a closer relationship with Him, and in some situations even salvation.

I have a friend we will call Dan. He had worked hard his entire life, was well established in the community and had a comfortable lifestyle. Yet for some reason had always shunned religion of any kind, comforting himself in believing he could eventually overcome any obstacle life threw at him.

Then that one thing he could not defeat came for a visit. Cancer, inoperable, and without mercy attached itself to him. He went through Chemo, Radiation, and dietary change, all to no avail.

Dan's sister suggested he make contact with her pastor. With some hesitation he did so. We spent numerous hours together discussing the things of God and eternity. On one of these occasions, I asked Dan if he would like Jesus Christ to forgive his sins, and receive the gift of eternal life? His answer was the same as I have heard numerous times before. "I have done some terrible things in my life and don't deserve forgiveness and the promise of heaven." I told him none of us deserved forgiveness and an eternity with God, but that God had sent His Son Jesus Christ into this world for people just like him, who had done "terrible" things in life. That day Dan received Jesus Christ as Savior and Lord. Three months later I was asked by his sister and family to preside at this funeral. Dan died of the cancer which had destroyed his body. God never healed him of the cancer. Healing did come to him when he placed his hand in a nail scarred hand and heard the words of His Savior welcome him home.

Did God cause Dan to get cancer. Of course not! God did use the cancer as a means of getting him to heaven. Keep in mind, Dan would have eventually died, cancer or no cancer. His cancer allowed him to see God in a way he had never seen Him before. In one sense, cancer was his introduction to a very real eternity he had run from and ignored his whole life.

Even though God did not heal my friend Dan, I have witnessed numerous occasions when He did do some miraculous healing. Individuals with sickness, life threatening injuries from accidents, birth defects, and yes, even self-imposed diseases like drug addiction and alcohol dependency.

I have another friend who had just graduated from college and was slated to begin a job he had only dreamed about. At the end of a Saturday night celebration, he made the decision to drive home, even though he had consumed way too much alcohol. He met another car in a head on collision. The passenger in the other car sustained some non-life-threatening injuries. My friend was not so fortunate. He was life flighted to a hospital trauma center, where the doctors gave his parents and fiancée little hope of recovery.

He did eventually recover though. After six months in a hospital, he was released. Unfortunately, he left with only one arm. The other being amputated because of the accident.

I had the unique opportunity to spend countless hours with him after he was released from the hospital. He carried a heavy load of guilt, and self-remorse for his actions. Because his over consumption of alcohol had led to the results he was now living with, he made a decision to never touch it again, in any form. There came a day in which he was able to ask God for forgiveness. With great humility, his parents, fiancée and even the person involved in the other car were also asked for forgiveness. He made a decision to tell his story to other young people who might be tempted to follow in his pre-accident days.

Today, now the father of three children, and a beautiful wife he has told his story to hundreds. Only time and eternity will tell of how the sharing of his story will have helped others to not make wrong decisions. Especially when drugs and alcohol are involved.

Did God cause the accident? Certainly not! Could He have prevented the accident from ever happening? Yes, He could have, after all He is God, and all things are in His power! But He did not. Questions like these are beyond our measured understanding of Divine sovereignty. Suffice to say, countless young lives are hearing a story that just could have been theirs. Each of them will remember the very real consequences of poor choices, as well as the healing and abiding presence of an Almighty God.

In both stories, God did do the work of healing. Not necessarily in the way we would have wished or even thought possible, but in such a way as to bring true and authentic healing. God is far more interested in our eternity than He is in our present. That in no way diminishes His considerable ability to intervene in our lives on a daily basis.

Today, if you are finding yourself in a difficult place, remember,

God can bring good and even great things out of the chaos of bad choices and decisions. Trust Him!

This concludes the writing with my friend Harlan! I hope you have enjoyed the journey as much as I have. My sole regret is that I did not finish my part while he was still alive. I miss his laughter, the keen insights to life which were individually his, and his gentle direction on things of the Spirit!

If there is any one thing, I can leave you with, it might be this; Treasure the friendships which make you better, and never procrastinate about things which you will never be able to re-visit!

As a final tribute to Harlan White, his complete writings, unedited are now provided for your reading pleasure.

13 WORDS UNSPOKEN

Poems and Writings by Harlan White

DEDICATED TO:

Doctors Carol Padilla and Lauren Ruby

Last year I found myself at the Veterans Hospital. What brought me here? The same circumstances that brought you here. Desperation. Frustration. Hopelessness. Oh yes, and one other crucial element, a hero brought me and stayed with me until I had enough information to make a decision about enrolling in treatment. Someone who had been here ahead of me. Do I know his name? I don't think I remember it. Why did he do that? He understood what you and I understand but can't find a way to explain or get passed.

Let me make this perfectly clear. I hated treatment. I hated every moment. The treatment was more than I believed possible for a human being to endure. In fact, I did not make it completely through my prescribed treatment. Nevertheless, during the months since, I have found something happening inside of me that I can't easily explain away.

Defining that "something" is more difficult. Maybe I can't accurately define it but I can say in reflection that it started here, here at the Veterans Hospital.

My downward spiral plateaued here, I hit with such force and pain that I could not recover my consciousness for a while. In truth, I didn't know if I ever would.

Since my treatment, I have awakened to my own self-destruction. So now what? If I do acknowledge that the thoughts I live in; the negative, destructive thoughts that represent my entire thinking process are killing me, I am more horrified than ever because I don't have a clue how or with what to replace them. Where do I begin? Is it too late to change? Is it worth the effort? I suppose my hero thought that there was hope.

Today, my self-destructive thoughts do not enjoy as much freedom as they once did. They do come with regularity but not without question. Where my solid internal sure-fire answers to all things resided, I now find the ability to question, to contemplate, to allow myself to take in knowledge. Somehow, I have found wonderment and dreams again. Only you can appreciate what a miracle this is.

My bedrock, my innermost foundation is in the process of rebuilding. Could it be some things are positive? I am not as terrified as I was and day by day I am escaping my inner world of terror replacing it with possibilities.

Yes, just like you I have experienced many tragedies. I mourn the losses of my life. While I am nor trying to forget or diminish those experiences, I am trying to include some other factors. I am practicing another focus. It doesn't seem natural just yet but there are many things I could appreciate. There are many things in my life that bring a sense of gratitude when I think to go there. I'm still practicing. I think that I will always be practicing.

Maybe because I am a carpenter, I think of my mind as having a workbench in it. On my mental workbench I have moved some things over that were taking up all the space and I have put some other things on that workbench. Looking here at other things, I amazingly find some rest and peace. I am learning from the bottom up, and that I must find a way to love and heal myself.

The principle that I continue to find amazing is this. The only way out of my internal prison is to give-a-little. Give a little each day, don't give away too much, but give a little every day.

Am I still overwhelmed? Do I still feel too small to deal with life every day? Yes. Yes. Yes. But I'm not thinking about that at this moment. I am thinking about giving a little today. That's what this is all about. Although I do not fully understand what happened to me at the Veterans Hospital, I know that something started in me here and I must acknowledge that process. I have a need to show my gratitude. Maybe it's just plain good manners- - I need to say "thank you" I need to say "thank you" to the hero that brought me here Thank you for hope when I couldn't find it for myself.

MAY YOU FIND A STOPPING POINT HERE. MAY YOU FIND A FLICKER OF LIGHT IN THE DARKNESS OF YOUR SOUL. ALTHOUGH YOU MAY FIND THIS THE DARKEST HOUR OF YOUR LIFE - - REMEMBER- - OTHERS HAVE WALKED BEFORE YOU AND WE ARE HOLDING YOU IN OUR HEARTS. HOLDING YOU IN THE SAME HOPE THAT SOMEONE HELD US. HOLDING YOU THROUGH THE PAIN THAT YOU'RE GOING THROUGH RIGHT NOW. BEYOND THE PAIN AMAZING DISCOVERIES ARE WAITING TO BE MADE AND BEHIND EACH DISCOVERY IS A SECRET. IN WONDERMENT AND DREAMS, YOU WILL FIND CLUES TO YOUR SECRETS.

Set Free

14 INTRODUCTION TO HARLAN'S POEM'S AND THOUGHTS

1 About War

2 Can't Get It Right

3 Chance

4 Choices

5 Compulsive Reality

6 Dyslexic Positive Thinking

7 Eternal Fathers

8 Fatherhood

9 Forever and Ever

10 Genesis 3

11 Good Chuck

12 Grandmother-Granddaughter

13 Greatness

14 Growing Up At The Gate

15 Growing Up On The Side Of The Hill

16 Highway To Hell

17 Humans On An Evil Stage

18 Learning 101

19 Life Is A Poem

20 Melancholy Blues

21 Mentor

22 Mirage

23 Monster Seed

24 My Life

25 Ode To A Bug

26 One More Day

27 Our Fate

28 Paradise Lake

29 Pink Clouds And Purple Skies

30 Pirates Bay

31 Poetic Purse

32 Pray For Today

33 Pressing on

34 Prize Fighter

35 Rebecca Jean

36 Run Doggie Run

37 The Door

38 The Missing Heart

39 The Nature of Things

40 The Songbirds Hymn

41 The Sword and The Cross

42 The Treehouse Tree

43 The Two Horse Sleigh

44 The Year 2K

45 Why

46 Writings

ABOUT WAR

Anyone who says the Vietnam War is over

Is either speaking from the grave or they weren't there!

Many are still fighting it.

Many are still dying.

The enemy we fought is as elusive today

As he always was

A soldier who loses a war

Is either dead or dying from it!

Only they who win can put it behind them.

The rest are doomed to an eternal fight!

Those who don't know, won't agree

Those who do, will!

H.D.W.

8-28-2000

CAN'T GET IT RIGHT

Can't write tonight

Can't say what is there

For every step

There seems to be a snare

I chose a path

All my doing

Still searching

Still pursuing

Learning much

With little gain

Great or small

Mistakes cause pain.

Footsteps in the drums of time.

Equal bondage freedom chimes.

Desolate in the mind which seeks

Escape from its own destiny.

Marching, longing to be free.

H.D.W.

CHANCE

You can read the cards

You can play the cards

But you can't read the cards that haven't been played

You can predict

You can guess

But what comes up is what you must play

The game is chance.

The game is luck

But if you lose you still must pay.

What you know

And what you think

You know may be to your advance

But in the end

What you thought you knew,

Still comes down to chance.

H.D.W.

CHOICES

There is in every thought, a decision to be made.

There is in every hand, two ways it can be played.

There is in every lie, a reason to be sad.

There is in every question, an answer to be had.

There is in every story, two ways it can be told.

There is in every journey, a fork in the road.

H.D.W.

COMPULSIVE REALITY

When an addiction is young, its owner is strong

As the addiction grows, its owner weakens

As the owner weakens and the addiction grows,

A transfer of power occurs

It's owners loss of power will be commensurate with

The addictions increase of strength

Never, will there be a balance of power, for the two cannot coexist!

One or the other by their very nature must and will always, without fail, conquer the other.

H.D.W.

DYSLEXIC POSITIVE THINKING

Never say what you mean.

Never mean what you say.

Nothing is your fault, others must pay.

Never let honesty get in your way.

Principles come second to purpose you know.

Hold back your friends and don't let them grow.

Sooner or later they'll weaken. That's when you

deal them your very best double-dealin' blow.

When they recover and see what you've done.

You just deny everything and have some fun!

H.D.W.

ETERNAL FATHERS

No darkness can hide me from you. If I took up the wings of an eagle,

You would already know my course.

Even in my own doings

My soul reports back to you.

Your greatness is unfathomable.

All of my life you have shown me a straight path.

You have led me to a road upward

That I avoid the shoals underneath.

Who am I that You who made the cedars of Lebanon

Should call me to mind?

Your greatness is beyond the understanding of one lifetime.

You have been gracious to me.

Tho the thistle has been in the drunkards hand

And the proverb in the fools mouth,

You have shown me mercy.

Never have I suffered from need or begged for bread.

I cannot see your face, but I can feel your hand upon me.

In times of trouble you are always there.

Set Free

In times of danger your footsteps precede mine.

Your protection is with me day and night,

Always you are by my side.

You govern the universe by Your will,

While the heavens display your handiwork.

In the sanctuary of your glorious might,

The planets and the stars maintain their paths

The seasons of earth rotate in order,

As do the seasons of man.

Until the silver cord has snapped

And I have traveled to my eternal home.

Until my dust returns to earth and my spirit returns to You,

I will praise You for my redemption

And trust in your steadfast love.

H.D.W.

FATHERHOOD

To be a father is to give life to a child.

To be a Dad is to occupy some of a child's life.

To be a PaPa is to be all the things a Father and a Dad wanted to be,

Were expected to be, could have been, should have been,

Were suppose to be.

Where, who, how does a boy go from boy to PaPa?

Where is the map? Who shows the way?

How do you go from one to another?

A Mother endures an insufferable amount of pain giving life!

There is another kind of pain involved in giving life that is silent,

Unseen, unappreciated and misunderstood

Mother is always Mother.

Father or Dad may or may not be.

H.D.W.

FOREVER AND EVER

The scene was solemn and the light just a glow.

I wasn't noticed, no one seemed to know

That I was disoriented and didn't have a clue where to go.

So faking a smile I stopped one sad faced old fellow.

What am I doing and why am I here?

When he looked up to respond, the hot wind dried his tears

This is forever

Forever what, I asked.

Forever and ever, now tend to your task.

I'm new here, I said, pardon me if I ask.

What is my purpose and what is my task?

Your purpose is on purpose, you chose to be here,

As far as a pardon, there's no such thing I fear.

Your task is to make ready for the wedding that will be

You will set placed throughout eternity.

You'll shine each gold plate and polish each cup.

But Sir, may I interrupt?

What's all this for?

Forever and forever, don't ask anymore

Set Free

What you're doing is your own doing

What you're doing is your own undoing,

You're here, is that clear?

You were invited to be part of the feast,

But you chose not to hear, they received no R.S.V.P.

You did nothing when you had the chance.

Nothing has produced nothing, so nothing you are.

You're nothing to me or anyone here

We're nothing to each other.

Wait a damn minute, you can't do this to me!

You did it to yourself, do you like what you see?

Polish those plates until they shine in your face,

Then look as you set the table and remember

Your choices you made in life

H.D.W.

GENESIS: 3

Would we be in this mess if Adam had confessed and just said, 'Oh Lord I've sinned. You made me master of all upon the earth and in the skies and in the seas. Like Yourself did you make me? From dust was I made and from my rib was my wife made. You did all this successfully. But, what I don't understand is how after we've been so close, You can hold this one mistake against me? You made the garden and You put me in charge and said 'don't eat of that tree' but You also made the snake who set me up for what was soon to be.

I didn't know death or sin or shame. I didn't know right from wrong and with one mistake You cast me out. That seems a little to strong.

I've done well with all you've given and all my responsibilities. I don't think it's right for you to condemn me, my wife and every one of my seed. I made a mistake. I made a bad choice. A bad moral choice, Indeed. But You are Divine and I am not. That's a lot of difference to me.

Now You blame my wife, You blame the snake and put the rest on me. I admit my part. I now know "wrong," and it all seems "wrong" to me. To blame all three of us and all people ever to be. You put that tree in front of us when all things you could see.

You knew what would happen and how it would go. How it would affect history. Isn't knowing good from evil punishment enough for eating from one bad tree? Remember in the mornings in the garden we'd walk, when it was only You and me?

You loved me so much, we shared so much...now death is what it must be?

If you were a man and I was god, I'd create some mercy for me. I would say that I forgive, and that forevermore forgiveness would replace that old tree. Then I'd write Genesis 3.

God answered Adam quietly. "Adam, I agree. I cannot undo what has been done, but my Son will rewrite Genesis 3. He'll fill the void and bridge the gap that now separates you and Me. And like you Adam, he'll face a test from a different kind of tree.

A price must be paid for what has been done. That's the way I caused things to be. I did it that way because as each price is paid another step is made towards a perfect eternity. You're the beginning of something much greater than yourself. Much greater than you can conceive

When you tasted the fruit of knowledge you opened a door for

Me. This battle for good and evil has raged through eternity.

In you I created a battlefield where I can conquer evil completely.

When I created "choice" I created something that was new to even

Me. We'll be together forever, Adam, you just wait and see. We've

been temporarily separated by death because of that 'ole tree

One day we'll be united again on a hill....Calvary....your seed

My Son and Me."

H.D.W.

3-23-1999

GOOD CHUCK

How much good, could a good dude do,

if a good dude would do good?

If what he didn't want to do,

was not what he didn't would anyone see what was done?

Would the high ideals of a prudent attempt,

out weigh the trickery he's bound to confront?

Would his heroism fade with the mess he had made

when his faults he was forced to confront?

When he failed would he say that

it wasn't his day or did a shooting star just go by?

If he could blind one eye to what he did askew,

would the other eye see what went right?

Could he possibly conceive that what he did

was achieve?

Could the good that he'd done when he carried more than one

be his comfort when the pendulum swung?

Could he ever go so wrong that all of his reference points

were gone?

Should he forge through the dark trusting the new day

Set Free

for the dawn?

If he chose to dive deeper than anyone had

in what he had set for his goal.

Could the bubbles of life surpass his endurance

and collapse what was left of his soul

Or would courage in it's most natural form,

Be the beginning of the upward assent?

Holding on is most often the lesser of valor

but often the best way to go!

H.D.W.

Grandmother/Granddaughter

There was a grandmother named Emma

who had a granddaughter named Gemma

Though others she had

none made her heart glad,

like the times she spent with Gemma

They would talk while they cooked

about trips that they'd took

about farm life, town life and neighbors

But nothing was said 'til Emma was dead

about how she had come to love Gemma

Grandmother, Granddaughter

with names just the same

One letter changed Grandmother

to granddaughter

When Gemma was told,

The "G" turned to gold

Now Gemma knew how Emma-got her!

We all see Emma in Gemma

H.D.W.

GREATNESS

Where lies the value in a man's life?

How is greatness achieved?

Does killing six million Jews make a mad German

greater than any one of his victims?

Will the annihilation of an entire Indian

nation bestow greatness on the one who leads the attack?

Can accumulation of millions by the sweat of others

give a man more value than what little his mother

might have seen in him?

Does the lust for power that supersedes human compassion

raise a man's true worth even one notch?

The measure of a man's worth, his success in life,

his value as a human being is always calculated in what good he

has done, who he has helped, what he has built.

Man is not measured by what he destroys but by what he

constructs!

What he puts back together what he mends, what he heals, and

what he touches with love.

H.D.W.

GROWING UP AT THE GATE

Blame on the kid on the stoop with the stick in his hand.

Sitting in the doorway, feet in the dirt.

Drawing lines in the dust. He drew the horse, then drew the barn.

He drew the windmill with particular form.

He'd scratch it out, then scratch his head.

then scratch some more until time for bed.

There was another boy, living in the same walls

Who didn't see the door with the kid on the stoop with the stick in

his hand.

Laying on the bed with a book in his hand,

he saw Tom and Huckleberry and Indian Jim.

He saw the bears and pigs and he heard the boy cry "wolf."

He tasted gingerbread with Hansel & Gretel.

He helped the pancake man across the street.

The kid who sat in the doorway, feet in the dirt,

drawing in the dust, saw his knees grow further from his chest.

He saw his pant legs shrink.

He remembered the shot with the grain of sand

that released the ant of its burden from five feet away.

Set Free

He was good!

The boy with the book in his hand, learned to let his mind expand.

He learned to see the good in what seemed all bad

He learned to see the bad in what seemed to be all good.

He learned everything he could.

They both grew old. They both went to heaven.

Waiting their turn at the pearly gates,

one was told to enter, the other to wait.

The one who had entered looked back at the other

and said to the Keeper, "Let him in, that's my brother"

H.D.W.

GROWING UP ON THE SIDE OF THE HILL

Wasn't it pleasant, O brother of mine when we lived on the side

of the hill? I shall never forget those days.

The cool of the old spring house. You older and somewhat

bolder and I the younger louse.

The Sunday's we dined on biscuits and gravy; the friends I don't

recall now. The sweet Mom sometimes made the peach marmalade:

the berries, the chiggers, the fun. The long summer days, the work in

the field and the quiet of the slow setting sun.

Wasn't it good for a boy to see—wasn't it good for a boy to be—

Growing up on the side of the hill?

Remember the hearts we broke in the fields when no one was there

but us? Devouring the center, leaving the rest for the hogs to eat in

the dust. The days seemed hard, the meat cooked in lard, the wood

we would cut to stay warm.

When the chores were through, when the darkness grew, and the

Lamp played scenes on the wall. Wasn't it pleasant, O brother

Of mine, when we had the chance to be boys.

How grateful I am for what we had then, growing up on the side of the hill. The times we had, the stern voice of Dad, the cream from the old milk cow. It's still clear in my mind. We'd reminisce about all this, if you were still here right now.

Wasn't it great, O brother of mine, growing up on the side of the hill.

Wasn't it pleasant for a boy to see—wasn't it good for a boy to be—growing up on the side of the hill.

H.D.W.

HIGHWAY TO HELL

I thumbed a ride after walking the road,

Should I have walked? Should I have road?

The destination is the same on the highway to hell.

It twists and turns, and goes mostly down.

There are no stops, there are no towns.

The only signal on the road is a clock.

Tick tock, tick tock.

Should I ride or should I walk?

Tick tock, Tick tock.

Your destination is your kind of fun?

When you arrive they'll say welcome son.

When the rest are settling at the great supper table,

Don't whine and say you were unable.

Now is your chance, now make your move.

You have the option to win or lose!

Tick tock, tick tock.

H.D.W.

HUMANS ON AN EVIL STAGE

Humans on an evil stage,

Doing man's inhumanity to himself.

No surprise, Mr. Death, I'm busy chasing wealth.

A line there is which crosses

before and after this,

and somehow, what we cannot see reacts to our remiss.

The land remains as though it were

While dust returns to dust.

The stage revolves around the sun with no influence from us

To fight there seems no option.

Struggle reigns supreme

To fight for what, for what to fight, lies squarely in between.

H.D.W.

"LEARNING" # 101

Peering into the mirror of life, glimpsing the fleeting ghosts,

I realize the things I've always done are the things I should have shunned the most.

The things I did and did so well, no longer make me boast.

My hero would be me today had I learned what I was taught.

But teaching one who will not learn, is tying two slip knots!

Not only does a fool not learn, but doesn't have a clue.

And when you've convinced the teacher and he believes in you,

Congratulations, the student is the teacher cause he's as dumb as You!

H.D.W.

LIFE IS A POEM

Standing in life one day

While looking at the sky,

I happened by chance a poem go by.

The poem grew so sad i began to cry.

I cried when it was over and as it went by.

I cried for the person and their plight.

I cried for their situation most of the night.

I longed to help and make their life better.

When they were lonesome I searched for the right letter.

What I wanted to say came way too late.

For the words of the poem had long sealed their fate.

I'm happy I got this glimpse as it went by,

But to care and not say is to flap and not fly.

I cried right up until dawn.

Then I cried because it was gone.

I cried not for myself but for what

I could not do to make life better for even these few.

All of the crying was perhaps in vain....

For why should one cry for another's past pain?

Set Free

So in the morning my mourning I ceased.

I put back the book and I erased the crease.

I thought of all the poems that would all pass me by.

I felt for each one, but, this time I didn't cry.

Life is a poem as each day goes by.

Sometimes we must laugh so we do not cry.

H.D.W.

MELANCHOLY BLUES

Today is another day. It is raining. The thunder brings back ghosts of another time.

I am strong. But my strength takes me to places I've already conquered. They are few.

I will meet life today with all its expectations. I will do what I must do, as honorably as I am able.

I will try, as best I can, to feel. I will try to feel something not associated with anger.

I will be the peaceful person I wish to project. However, I will survive.

I will overcome all apparent adversities. I will reach inside myself and extract what is required to survive or exist.

I will display love, as I see it, to those closest to me! If I error, I will apologize.

I will concur, as closely as possible, to what I interpret as sociably correct.

I will seek a Higher Power, which I neither know or understand!

Each year of my life is one trip around the sun. I will make as many trips as are required of me, doing as little harm as I can to others as they make their journey.

If I have the opportunity to help someone along the way,

I will do it without reimbursement.

I will experience happiness, joy, peace and fulfillment.

Set Free

I will be happy if it kills me!

I'm being positive, I'm sure of it!

The things I like most are:

BIG FISH

LITTLE KIDS

TALL TRUCKS

SHORT STORIES

LONG NAPS

SKINNY GIRLS

FAT (ON PRIME RIB)

AND YOU!

H.D.W.

MENTOR

In the soul there lives a knowledge deep within us all,

That pulls us all together, yet separates us all.

Some men climb the highest mountains only for the test.

Some men search the deepest ocean for what the past has left.

The future lies before us, three choices there may be.

To live again;

To live no more.

To live eternally.

He who taught me, searched through life with diligence his best,

To leave with me and all his seed, to what he must attest.

For what he found to be the way deep within me knows,

His life has spent confirming the "Rose of Sharon" road.

The path with which he chose to trod through life ultimately will be,

The path that takes each one of us to life eternally!

H.D.W.

MIRAGE

It rolled and it rolled 'til it rolled right by.

When I was high I laughed.

When I wasn't, I cried.

Once it seemed eternal infinite in scope.

Then it occurred to late it was the mirage of the dope.

What I thought lay ahead was not what was there.

What I once saw as hope at a closer look was despair.

It rolled and rolled "till it rolled right by.

As age consumed youth, I continued to fly.

I soared above life with no altitude

Most of the soaring done in a bad mood.

It rolled and it rolled 'til it rolled right by.

It rolled right up 'til the time to die

It rolled way beyond the time to ask why.

I laughed when I was high

When I wasn't I cried!

H.D.W.

MONSTER SEED

A MONSTER was created! In my mind he was conceived!

From hell he got permission to grow and deceive!

And though I knew much better

To this I did agree.

Feed me, said the MONSTER! To this you must agree.

For are you not obligated to feed that which you have conceived?

And though I knew much better,

To this I did agree.

The MONSTER grew much faster than you would believe.

By now he could lie and he could deceive.

And though I knew much better,

To this I did agree.

LEAVE! I told the MONSTER for you are not part of me.

No! Roared the MONSTER my home is where I was conceived.

And though I knew much better,

To this I did agree.

The MONSTER grew so large inside of me as did his hellish greed

that I spent wasted years trying to meet my MONSTER'S need

And though I knew much better,

To this I did agree.

I have nothing left to give you, all my thoughts you now control.

The MONSTER said there is still something that has always been my goal.

NOW I WILL REQUIRE YOUR SOUL.

And though I knew much better............

H.D.W.

MY LIFE

Of all the spooks

I've met in my life

Not one was ever a ghost.

Of all the bridges

I've burned in my life,

Not one was a weeny-roast.

Of all the things

I've lost in my life

I miss my mind the most.

H.D.W.

"ODE TO A BUG"

Spiders and slugs

and all kinds of bugs

come crawling around my door.

They crawl up my wall

And some of them fall.

Some just stay on the floor.

Some are really ugly.

Some are quite cute.

One even tried to eat my wool suit.

But of all the bugs

that i ever knew,

Some green, some black, some blue

The loveliest bug

I ever saw

died crawling out of my shoe!

H.D.W.

ONE MORE DAY

Just one more day, Oh Lord I pray,

Before this man turns back to clay.

So many things I need to say,

so many debts I must repay!

You've blessed us all;

I more than most

Bless this breakfast and this burnt toast.

Make this day by far the best

and may I drive without arrest.

Search my heart and not my car.

Love my kids the way they are.

Just one more day and then I'll pay.

That's just two days from yesterday.

H.D.W.

OUR FATE

To live in democracy is to live in mediocrity. America, don't turn from God!

The church is the conscience of the state. The choice we all call "our fate."

America is a republic of law. There's no moral conscience to control our incompetence,

Then let's all be heathens and sexual deviants and watch the lions take control.

The state without a church is a bird without a perch.

If we follow each other without the church as our mother and disregard what we know,

then Clinton will be the best we'll ever see and God's plan will have failed us all.

Lucifer will prevail, we'll all live in hell. Human nature can take its free will.

"But for me and my house, we'll serve the Lord" and "to hell" with Hilary and Bill???

Light dispels darkness or it exists under a bushel. Which even light is still light.

Truth will be truth. Love will still love. Regardless of our politics.

So let's let our light shine in our "day and time."

Let evil play its tricks on itself. Let he who did nor fall be a role model for us all.

Or let's empower a fool. He left us the choice… that's the purpose of our life.

Our choice even He cannot call.

If I were a senator in Solomon's court, I would propose a "New Bill."

This Bill would make Christ the speaker of the house and Senior Presiding Resident.

Dad would replace Newt, Reno would go and Mom would be "President."

H.D.W.

PARADISE LAKE

In a dream I stood at the edge of an unearthly magnificent lake.

The water so clear it reflected the sun.

Sparkling crystals of aqua blue water took my breath away.

In the distance, I saw a dock and a marina filled with brand new fishing boats.

I reached the dock after a lovely walk and met one white-haired old gentleman.

He smiled and I caught a twinkle in his eye as he greeted me.

Good morning my fellow fishing friend, calling me by name.

Welcome to Paradise Lake.

Trying to hide my surprise, I returned his smile and asked him about this heavenly place.

He began a story about the lake that started at the beginning of time.

This lake was created for real down to earth fishermen, those like you and I.

There's plenty of fish of every kind.

The minnows are six inches long.

We have Bass, Largemouth and Browns, Crappie, Walleye, Cats of all kinds, Bullheads, Channel, Flatheads and Blues, Muskie, Pike and Salmon.

You name it, we have it too.

Set Free

I asked about the tackle and what a man would use.

He seemed amused by my choice of words, such as what a man would use,

But politely continued and reached for a pole lying on the dock.

We use these, he said, presenting a golden rod made of a material totally unfamiliar to me.

The length expands and contracts depending on it's use.

The line on that reel never breaks and those hooks have never been known to bend or dull.

When I inquired about such boats, he led me a few slips down the dock.

That's not fiberglass son, that's father-of-pearl.

It never cracks.

A rock struck solid won't even leave a scratch.

Seeing no motor, I naively asked, what makes her go?

You do, he said.

She'll go as fast as you will her to go.

I noticed the bow had no numbers, and then to my surprise,

my full name written in silver was scrolled on her side!

Sure is, he said, that one's yours.

It's been here since the beginning of time.

Embarrassed by my excitement, I said, can we take her for a spin?

Set Free

His voice softened as he spoke, Not today, my friend.

I noticed other boats with other names nearby;

Simon, James, John....

With his hand on my shoulder, he led me off the dock.

You'd better go now, you don't belong here yet.

With great reluctance, I complied and started back down the shore.

One last question sir, How will I find you when I return?

Again, I saw that twinkle in his eye.

Ask for Peter, I'm well known around here.

Then, we said goodbye.

As the alarm clock rang, I sat up with a smile, ready to rise and shine.

What is it dear? My woman asked. Oh, nothing honey, I replied.

I was just thinking about an old friend of mine.

H.D.W.

PINK CLOUDS AND PURPLE SKIES

Pink clouds and purple skies surround the mountains in her mind

She closes her eyes.

She's dancing

The breeze from the top is exhilarating.

The wind fills her wings,

She's flying.

Musical currents in time like thermals give lift to her heart

The sun is shining. Her heart full of joy,

sings from the highest peak.

She's loving.

Without warning , darkness and fear cover her world.

She's falling, twisting and turning. Spiraling out of control.

She looks within herself for an answer. There is none.

Tranquility and peace lay below her in the valley that so quickly welcomes her arrival.

She's lonesome.

Her breath eludes her. Her lungs collapse.

Laying face down, hope trickles from her dreams. She's hurting.

The slightest gust creates a spark.

From a spark, a flame. From a flame, a fire.

She's burning

Feeling again, belonging again. She's living from the mountain so high to her....

they beckon to climb. She hesitates. She knows....

I'm always on the mountain when I fall.

H.D.W.

PIRATES BAY

Down the road we went just you and I, buying minnows along the way.

Listening to you, how you already knew the big one's would be biting today.

With tangled poles we share our souls down at Pirates Bay.

I miss my mama, but daddy's there, I know everything is ok.

So watch out PAPA, just bait my hook and I'll be the first to say I got a bite, I got a fish, never mind he got away.

For one second of time we were the same age when we had that chance to play.

When I grow up will you come here with me and my son so I can say,

I taught Papa and I'll teach you how to catch fish here at Pirates Bay.

H.D.W.

POETIC PURSE

The key to the poetic purse is to shrink all the words

and maintain the verse.

What you say, say concise.

Keep your "personals" to your own devise.

If you maintain the meter, you focus the reader

and what you have said is precise.

H.D.W.

PRAY FOR TODAY

Precious is the mind that tallies up the good.

Alone brave soul stand; and stand there good.

Calculating, summing up, the negativity of time.

Seeing only evil focused on the crime.

Good there was in those who lost.

Though they be the Romans prey.

Twist not the lions tail!

But count the good today!

H.D.W.

PRESSING ON

My vulnerability made me fearful.

My fear turned to anger.

My anger turned to rage.

My rage, forced me to find help.

In help, I found God.

In God, I found hope.

In hope, I found life.

In life, I found love.

In love I found the part of me that I thought was missing.

H.D.W.

PRIZE FIGHTER

There's been only one in my life, who could live with the strife.

Who could smile on the gray cloudy days.

The only one with what it took, standing beside me,

to draw courage from her own life, so adverse.

Who could see through the bad, to the good that she had,

In the man with whom she'd spend her life.

To fight for that life and to be a good wife.

To stand, refusing to fall.

To fight round after round, simply by not going down.

Who would see the beauty of the dawn

long before the darkness left my eyes

My partner in life, my Prize Fighter,

my woman, my lover, my Wife.

H.D.W.

REBECCA JEAN

(Harlan made a notation on this poem- "Not to be used without permission").

There's a hole in our hearts and our flesh is weak to bear this untried pain.

But in the choir of heavens souls we know she now remains

We long for her household voice, for her smile and laugh, we long.

But "God" has led our Dear One on and He can do wrong!

We know not of His Islands which now she is a part.

We only know the part of her that lingers in our heart.

Oh Father, as she arrives on Your heavenly scene,

please accept her with our deepest love, our precious Rebecca Jean.

The family of Rebecca Jean

H.D.W.

RUN DOGGIE RUN

Run doggie run as fast as you can.

Run for the man with the wheel in his hand.

Run doggie run for the track is no puzzle.

Run doggie run in spite of the muzzle.

Run doggie run 'til the race is all done

A piece of the rabbit is better than none.

Run from the cabins; run for 'ole Doane.

You win this race and you'll be cloned.

Follow the string 'til the string is wound tight.

Run down the track with all of your might.

Run doggie run 'til you're lean and mean.

Run for the prize in 'ole Abilene.

H.D.W.

THE DOOR

So it's the unknown that we fear?

Though we live a life pure.

At the end, how can we really be sure?

Was our doing worth doing?

Was our effort worthwhile?

Is there really a wrong and a right?

Where grave rapture second life,

Has anyone been there before?

Where your going you must make the trip alone.

But the trip's been made many times.

Death is a door, not a rosy door,

But life isn't all daffodils.

Do you remember being born?

I suspect you were there.

Wasn't that an unknown door?

You made the trip, now you are there.

Now you worry about not being there.

Death is only another door.

H.D.W.

THE MISSING HEART

From my chair a sound warns me, footsteps crossing my porch.

I'd recognize them anywhere, it's the Burglars, they've been here before.

Two eyes peek in before entering, she comes in through the front door.

Hauling the treasures she brought with her and dumping them all on the floor.

From the kitchen a crash and a stumble, three marbles, two toys, one boy.

Our eyes meet with both of us grinning. My castle's been invaded with joy.

The one from the front approaches my chair presenting a sweet cheek to be kissed.

The following giggle always makes me wonder, was it me or my mustache that she missed?

I see that the boy is now hiding, he's lurking behind the far wall.

He's plotting to jump out and scare grandma when she carries their toys down the hall.

Soon my castle's entirely invaded, I've been taken hostage it seems.

But I'm temporarily released at the end of each day with a hug and a whisper "sweet dreams"

When the burglars have gone and the weekend has too and I still have my silver and gold.

I realize there is one thing missing…..It's grandpa's heart that they stole.

H.D.W.

THE NATURE OF THINGS

They said it would come. It did.

Though I doubted it, they're seldom right.

Distress for some comes with it. Even so,

it causes one to remember what peace there is in silence.

The trees were the first to know. They labor in noisy

confusion at its arrival. Throwing there leaves in the

air like so many sacrifices.

Perhaps the porch swing understood the truth

the trees knew. With its ardent banging against

the house. These sentinels seem to find achievement

in being the first to warn us.

The street light flickered, or did it wink?

Whichever, it was enough to expose the Exodus

the loose dirt near the curb was making

Somewhere a banging door set the cadence of the event.

The stars hid their twinkle behind courses

of thick black clouds.

A million man army of raindrops charged from

above and pelted every dry victim in their path.

Like a symphony whose conductor was cynical

about affection, it pounded relentlessly on the roof.

With little notice of its intent, it retreated. Then

It was gone. It's occurrence was never in doubt.

It leaves pools of evidence as proof

It's presence creates dark imaginings in our mind.

However, it has its place in the universe

no less than the trees and the stars.

Perhaps there is even virtue in its existence

However far beyond a wholesome discipline

it may seem to us to be!

H.D.W.

THE "SONGBIRD'S" HYMN

A day is a time from dawn 'til dark.

Life is a journey from birth to the park.

Both freely given, each ours to use.

Still belonging to him, not ours to abuse.

The Songbird's hymn at the end of day

Honors the Giver, the only required pay.

A life freely given, an opportunity to honor Him.

A chance to share the Songbird's hymn.

H.D.W.

THE SWORD AND THE CROSS

The sword was worn from battle, that was plain to see.

It lay upon a table marked....immortality.

With curious hands I touched the edge... it opened up to me.

There upon that table, I witnessed all eternity.

All the battles ever fought and all those yet to be.

Pointed back to just one day... the day at Calvary.

A form I saw upon a cross. The cross became a sword.

The blood that dripped from that sword became a living word.

The word became a fountain and offered me to drink.

I touched the blood to my lips. It said it was for me.

All of life and all of death depend upon Calvary.

H.D.W.

THE TREEHOUSE TREE

To some it meant the end.

A rope tied to a tree

To me it meant the best of times

swinging in the breeze.

Little toes reaching skyward,

blue skies reaching down to me.

Cherished childhood memories

still linger in that tree.

To tend to all the business of a treehouse maitre d'.

Tea and cookies on the menu, the first course, naturally.

Followed by endless ideas of what my life would be.

Grandma's house is the safest place I'm sure I'll ever be.

And all the treasures life could hold

couldn't equal that one tree.

Swing me higher this time Pa Pa,

so the whole world I can see.

Make my whole life just as grand

as it looks from Grandma's tree!

H.D.W.

THE TWO-HORSE SLEIGH

Say, have you heard of the wonderful two horse sleigh?

It was designed in such a wonderful way,

that only the perfect pair of horses could move that sleigh.

Nineteen hundred and forty-nine,

two young horses were paired at that time.

Shortly thereafter, they were hitched to the sleigh.

They moved that sleigh then and still could today.

Not especially a magical pair,

but to see them both work would cause folks to stare.

They pulled that sleigh in the ice and the mud,

they pulled it right through the fifty-one flood.

They pulled out of town called Lane one day;

there were now four attached to the sleigh.

Two of them pulling with colts by their side.

Were those colts ever in for a ride!

Together they galloped on towards destiny.

Which, by the way, let straight to K.C.

While in Kansas City, the mare added to the team... two more tiny ears.

It took lots of patience to handle that five,

Set Free

but to this day they all survived!

Said he to her, "I feel in my heart,

We should help others make a new start."

So down on Poplar, they open a stable,

designed to help horses who were disabled.

With undaunted spirits the two pulled that sleigh

clear through the fifties, side by side, all the way.

Said he to her, "We could pull more."

She sighed and took notice of the shoes her colts wore.

"I'll do my part to pull as I must,

In you and the Master, I've put my trust."

So, into the sixties they pulled a huge load,

the sleigh growing heavier, with the ruts in the road.

She'd glance at him as if to say,

could it be possible, we've overloaded this sleigh?

His head would rare, his nostrils would flair,

he'd pull even harder to ease the load of his mare.

She'd regain her footing and take up her load

and all through the seventies, they followed the road.

Did I tell you, or have you guessed, they were a wonder and

nothing less!

Set Free

Their colts grew to horses, some hair turned to gray.

Still they pulled steady on the two horse sleigh.

Clear through the eighties, still strong and sound,

pulling together, covering more ground.

One day in the nineties, he pulled to the side of the road

and said to those riding, "Now it's your load."

He looked at his mare and spit out his bit,

said "I know you're still strong, but gal this is IT!

Rest for awhile, this is our day.

We'll ride with the Master the rest of the way."

The story is true, fifty years to the day,

It takes many horses to pull that same sleigh!

H.D.W.

THE YEAR 2K

What if in the year 2K, we did the defense budget a different way?

Instead of missiles carrying nuclear warheads,

we financed hardware that could deliver bunk beds.

We could build rockets that delivered such things as medicine,

food and clothes.

We'd be the ones to get the bang out of those.

We could make tanks, artillery too,

that shot only lunchmeat, bologna and stew.

As for chemical weapons, we'd have a few,

but the chemicals would be to prevent colds and flu.

NASA could have its billions just as they must

but they would launch houses for fighting homelessness.

We could all have houses with warm cozy beds.

We'd each have a rifle that shoots loaves of bread

None of our weapons would do someone harm.

That kind of thing would all be "disarmed."

In this land of plenty, there's enough for us all,

if we just helped each other when someone takes a fall.

Minorities, majorities and poor folks too,

could have designer tennis shoes.

Uncle Sam would no longer point his finger at you

because he would now have something worthwhile to do.

He'd be so proud of me and you,

he'd wave boldly his red, white and blue.

H.D.W.

WHY

You are the best of my life.

You are the worst of my life.

Sometimes I ponder why

I ever agreed to be your wife.

Sometimes I think you love me.

Sometimes I think you don't.

The way changes from day to day.

And makes me feel like an old goat.

Sometimes you say things

that melt my heart.

Sometimes what you say

drives us apart.

What can I do?

What can I say

that will help you understand

what you really mean to say.

Is this for you?

Is this for me?

Why can't it be

the way it used to be.

H.D.W.

WRITINGS

When a man is running, is he running towards something? Is he running away from something? Can a man run just to keep from stalling?

When the earth and the sky are both on fire, where does the eagle land? Could it be he flies on just to keep from falling?

A funny thing happened when I last left town.

Inanimate objects began to leave the ground.

Ashtrays and glasses suddenly learned to fly

They whizzed through the air with a missile like cry.

Powder and cologne learned this trick too.

The difference between playing monopoly and real life is that when one person ends up with all the money in real life, you must keep playing.

I can see better behind me.

Every free spirit needs a tether.

Every bound soul needs release.

If the first beating a woman takes from a man is not the last, it's physical evidence of brain damage by the first!

What about a verbal beating?

H.D.W.